Sister

By Mildred Crofutt Bryant

"I am writing this, not to boast about anything I may have done, but to show that by working together, a family can beat the odds, especially with such kindly friends and neighbors as we had."

Sister
By Mildred Crofutt Bryant

Published by:
Bench Mark Enterprises
4450 California Avenue, Suite K123
Bakersfield, CA 93309
(800) 773-1570

All rights reserved. No part of this book may be reproduced or transmitted in any form or by any means, electronic or mechanical, including photocopying, recording or by any informational storage and retrieval system without written permission from the author, except for the inclusion of brief quotations in a review.

Copyright © 1999 by Mildred Crofutt Bryant

Edited by Eddy Communications, Bakersfield, California
Cover design and layout by McDuff Graphics, Bakersfield, California

Printed in the United States of America

Library of Congress Cataloging-In-Publication Data
Bryant, Mildred Crofutt
    Sister. 1st ed.
      1. Family history.   2. Wyoming history
      I. Bryant, Mildred Crofutt II. Title

ISBN 0-9652973-1-4   99-62004

I dedicate this book to our parents, Charley and Edith Crofutt, who instilled in us what it took to carry on after they were gone.

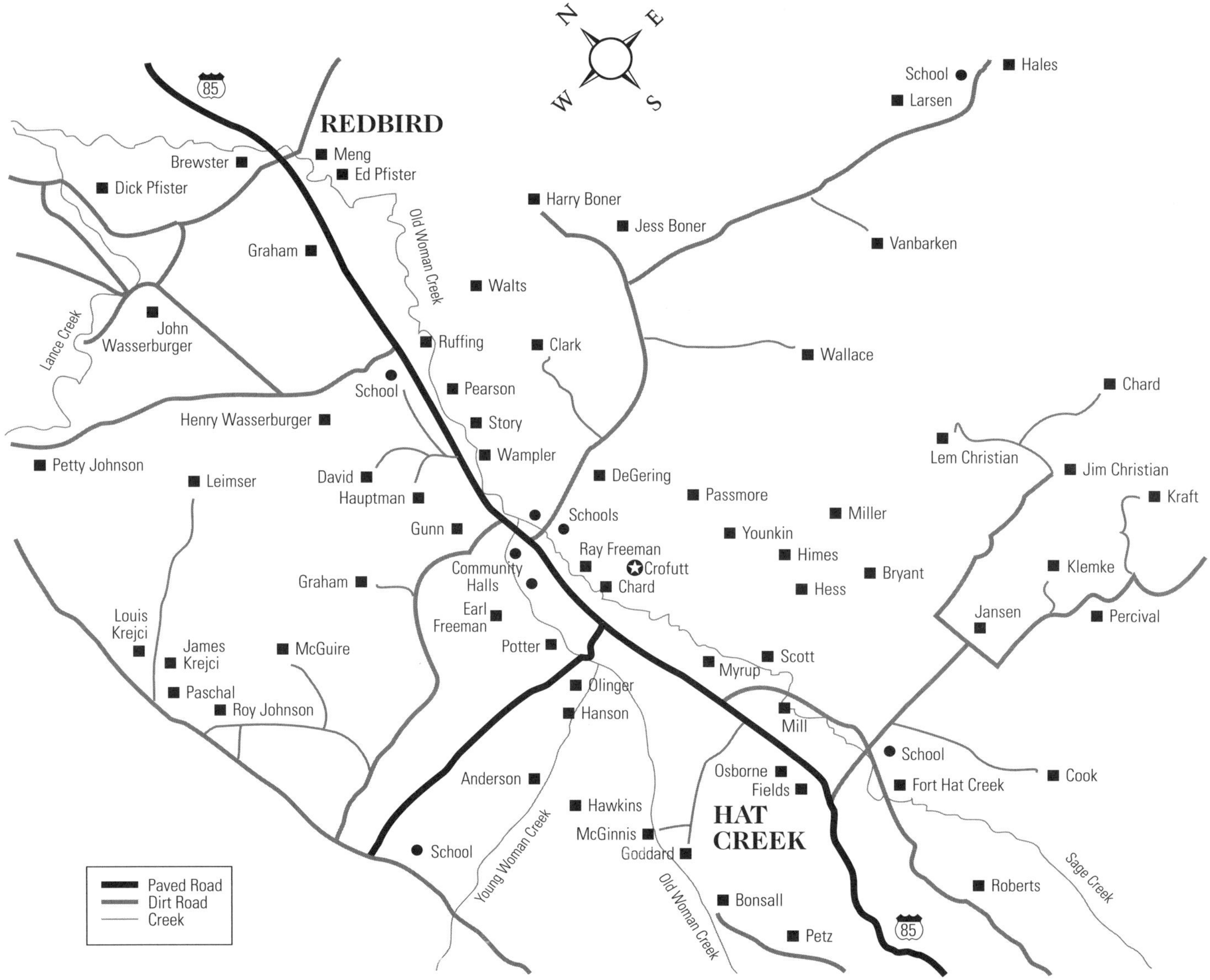
N
E
W
S
85
REDBIRD
Meng
Ed Pfister
Brewster
Dick Pfister
Graham
Old Woman Creek
Harry Boner
Jess Boner
School
Larsen
Hales
Vanbarken
Walts
Lance Creek
John Wasserburger
Ruffing
Clark
Wallace
School
Pearson
Henry Wasserburger
Story
Wampler
Chard
Lem Christian
Jim Christian
Kraft
Petty Johnson
Leimser
David
Hauptman
DeGering
Passmore
Miller
Schools
Gunn
Younkin
Ray Freeman
Crofutt
Himes
Bryant
Klemke
Graham
Community Halls
Chard
Hess
Earl Freeman
Jansen
Percival
Louis Krejci
James Krejci
McGuire
Potter
Scott
Myrup
Olinger
Paschal
Roy Johnson
Hanson
Mill
School
Cook
Anderson
Osborne
Fields
Fort Hat Creek
Hawkins
HAT CREEK
McGinnis
Goddard
School
Young Woman Creek
Old Woman Creek
Roberts
Sage Creek
Bonsall
Petz
85
Paved Road
Dirt Road
Creek

Table of Contents

Chapter 1
Our Roots, 1894 – 1922 1

Chapter 2
School Years, 1923 – 1938 15

Chapter 3
The Fire, 1938 41

Chapter 4
Carrying On, 1938 – 1941 49

Chapter 5
The War Years, 1941 – 1945 61

Chapter 6
Finally… 79

Foreword
By Lola Crofutt Leonard

I was three years old when my parents died, so Sister is the only mother I ever knew. (We always called her "Sister" because we couldn't say "Mildred." She remains "Sister" to this day.) Sister had just finished college to receive her teaching credential. Instead of anticipating her new career, she was faced with the responsibility of caring for seven of her brothers and sisters. She could have chosen to find all of us homes with relatives or other families. She chose to keep us all together and take on the awesome task of raising us.

Besides working to feed us, she also had to work to run a household for eight people. She said one of the hardest things was keeping everyone in shoes. Of course, the older kids helped so much, but for Glenn and me, Sister became our mother. She is a remarkable person and we should all be thankful to her for hanging in there for us.

My first memory was sitting on a blanket watching the fire that destroyed our home. Then our dad took Glenn and me to Ray Freeman's, a close neighbor. The fire caused the deaths of both my parents and a sister.

The neighbors in the area came to our aid and supplied our immediate needs. Later on, since I was not old enough to go to school, I went to stay with Margaret Chard while Sister taught school. During World War II, Gerald and Keith went into the service, so that left Lawrence, Enis and Iris to help out at home.

There were always chores to do when we got home from school. Cows had to be milked, chickens fed and eggs gathered before starting supper and we each had our own "chores" to do.

One time Glenn and I messed around until after dark to get the wood in. While Glenn chopped the wood, I picked up chips. I got too close and he hit me on the head with the axe. I can still see the look on Sister's face when I came in with blood running down my face. After that we got the wood in before dark.

I can clearly remember Sister frying potatoes and onions for supper, and me standing by the sink while she put curlers in my hair.

After Sister got married, we left "the place" (as we always called our homestead) and moved to Colorado. I was 11 years old at the time. When I was 15, I went back to Lusk so I could graduate from high school there. I never lived with Sister again after that, but since I was the youngest, I lived with her the longest.

Sister always had a strong sense of values. It was always understood we all would graduate from high school, and all eight of us did—all from the same school. That must have been a real job. Not all kids with parents can say that, but then they never had the caring, strong sister that we had.

To Mildred:

To have known you as a child and now as an adult is a pleasure and I see you as an example not only of love for your family, but also of patience and acceptance of people and responsibility. Many people may have wondered how you did it, but no one who knows you would wonder why.

~ Mary Jones
Cousin

Editor's Notes

In 1996, a trip to Wyoming had a bigger impact on me than I could have imagined. My father wanted to show me the new fence and other improvements recently completed on a small family cemetery located on my grandparents' ranch. The cemetery contains the graves of three of my father's siblings who died in infancy.

It was a hot summer day and a strong wind was whipping across the flat prairie as it often does in that area. I have been to that little cemetery many times, but on that day it became very real to me my grandmother went out on that desolate prairie and buried her babies in the hard ground among cactus and sagebrush. I was moved to tears, just thinking of all of the hardships endured by previous generations of my family. I knew the basic story of the many years of struggle; but, my dad and his siblings never complained about the hard years, so I never really knew the whole story. I wanted to know more and make a record so others could know the story as well.

I have come to admire my dad, Glenn, and all my aunts and uncles even more through helping my Aunt Mildred put this book together. I have grown a deep respect for a grandfather I never knew, who through great sacrifice wanted a better life for his own children and who knew the importance of an education that he never had. I am amazed at the hardships my grandmother must have endured, working to feed and clothe such a large family with very meager means. I also appreciate the character instilled in their children, which enabled them to go on in the face of their tragedy. One can only imagine how difficult it was just to survive and cope with the responsibilities before them.

I want to thank Kathy Eddy for all of her help. I couldn't have done it without her. Also, thank you to all the other special people who have made this book possible.

~ Cheree Crofutt Linford

Acknowledgements

Thanks to Freda Story and Ernie Wampler for sharing some of their memories. Thank you to Twila Barnette at the Stagecoach Museum in Lusk, Wyoming for giving me access to the newspaper archives, copying articles, lending support and encouragement, and to The Lusk Herald for permission to use these articles.

Thank you to my sister Lola Crofutt Leonard for writing such a kind foreward. Thank you to my sister Iris Crofutt Baughn for researching our family tree. Thank you to my brother Glenn Crofutt for reading and rereading the text to check for facts. Thank you to my brother Enis Crofutt for his support. Thank you to my cousin Mary Jones for her support.

Thank you to Cheree Crofutt Linford, Kathy Eddy, Robert McDuff and all the others who helped make this book possible. And finally, thank you to all the friends and neighbors, who are too numerous to name, who helped us over the years.

~ Mildred Crofutt Bryant

Our Family Tree – *Compiled by Iris Crofutt Baughn*

- **Josiah Crofutt** & **Rebecca Gregory**
  - **Ezra Crofutt**
    Born October 12, 1809, Susquehenna, PA
    Died September 15, 1892, Esbon, KS
- **John Park** & **Elizabeth Bingham**
  - **Olive Eudorah Park**
    Born September 8, 1832, New York State
    Died March 26, 1916, St. Cloud, MN
    - **Ira Elmer Crofutt**
      Born August 7, 1869, Grinnell, IA
      Married December 25, 1894, Springfield, SD
      Died March 14, 1949, Hot Springs, SD
- **Charles Henry Morton** & **Unknown**
  - **Charles Henry Morton**
    Born May 20, 1829, Austin, TX
    Married March 18, 1874, Springfield, SD
    Died March 18, 1914, Springfield, SD
- **Isaac (John) Enders** & **Martha Stevens**
  - **Lavilla Enders**
    Born February 23, 1857, Fort Dodge, IA
    Died March 28, 1950, Springfield, SD
    - **Henrietta Sopha Morton**
      Born December 21, 1877, Redbird, NB
      Died February 10, 1971, Custer, SD

- **Charles Elmer Crofutt**
  Born July 26, 1895, Guthrie Center, IA
  Married July 26, 1916, Alliance, NB
  Died May 26, 1938, Lusk, WY

Sister – Crofutt Family History

Edith Mary Lineback
Born
February 9, 1895
Broken Bow, NE
Married
July 26, 1916
Alliance, NB
Died
May 25, 1938
Lusk, WY

- **William Alford Lineback**
  Born
  August 31, 1865
  Peoria, IL
  Married
  May 23, 1888
  Weeping Water, NB
  Died
  Unknown
  - **Freeman Lineback**
    Born
    1838
    Indiana
    Married
    February 24, 1859
    Tazwell Co., IL
    Died
    March 22, 1867
    Peoria, IL
    - **William Lineback**
  - **Susan Richardson**
    Born
    August 25, 1843
    Illinois
    Died
    August 18, 1916
    Weeping Water, NB
    - **Elizabeth Weeks**

- **Millie Hardy**
  Born
  September 18, 1869
  Port Clinton, OH
  Died
  June 30, 1913
  Grand Island, NB
  - **Silas Adrian Hardy**
    Born
    May 20, 1840
    Erie, PA
    Died
    December 7, 1880
    Port Clinton, OH
  - **Anna Miller**
    Born
    January 10, 1848
    Ohio
    Died
    October 27, 1913
    Kearney, NB
    - **Jacob Miller**
    - **Catherine Kabler**

The Charles and Edith Crofutt Family

Charles Crofutt
Born July 26, 1895
Married July 26, 1916 at age 21
Died May 26, 1938 at age 42

Edith Lineback Crofutt
Born February 9, 1895
Married July 26, 1916 at age 21
Died May 25, 1938 at age 43

Children	Born	Died	Age at Time of Fire
Mildred	May 5, 1917, Ashby, NE	–	21
Gerald	February 19, 1919, Hat Creek, WY	1986	19
Faye	May 1920, Hat Creek, WY	(stillborn)	–
Lawrence	July 5, 1921, Hat Creek, WY	1994	16
Keith	November 30, 1922, Hat Creek, WY	December 20, 1944 (WWII)	15
Enis	April 17, 1925, Lusk, WY	–	13
Iris	May 19, 1926, Hat Creek, WY	–	12
(Ivah) Lois	August 20, 1928, Hat Creek, WY	May 24, 1938 (in fire)	9
Lyle	August 13, 1930, Hat Creek, WY	September 10, 1930	–
Glenn	January 27, 1932, Lusk, WY	–	6
Irma	April 18, 1933, Hat Creek, WY	September 1933	–
Lola	August 3, 1934, Hat Creek, WY	–	3

Chapter 1
Our Roots, 1894–1922

My grandparents, Ira Crofutt and Henrietta Morton met and married in Springfield, South Dakota, in 1894. My father Charley was born in Guthrie Center, Iowa, in 1895, but spent his early years in Springfield, South Dakota, along with three brothers and two sisters.

In 1907, Ira came to Nebraska, and in 1908, he homesteaded in northern Sheridan County. At this time, Henrietta and their six children, along with their stock and property, came from Springfield to Rushville, Nebraska, by train. They drove their wagons and stock to their homestead near the Spade ranch, where Ira would work for several years. Six more children were born there.

My grandparents farmed to make a living to supplement Ira's thirty dollar a month salary. The first summer they lived in a tent, then they built the dugout, which was partly on top of the ground. In 1910, they dug a well nearby, then built a sod house.

My father and his brothers and sisters attended school in a sod building on land given to them by the Spade ranch. Parents and ranch employees built the school. As soon as Charley was old enough he went to work on the ranch as a cowboy.

My father's family. Dad is back row, center with white shirt.

In 1915 Ira decided to take the family and move to Missouri. Charley stayed on to work at the Spade Ranch. In 1916 he married Edith Lineback, who had come to the ranch to work.

Edith's parents, William and Millie Lineback, came to southern Nebraska from Illinois and Ohio. They were married in Weeping Water, Nebraska on May 23, 1888. All of their twelve children were born in the area.

Edith was their fourth child, and was born on February 9, 1895 at Broken Bow, Nebraska. Her parents passed away when she was in her teens, and she and her younger brothers and sisters lived with a married brother Paul, and his wife, Ocia. Edith later went to work at the Spade Ranch, helping with cooking and housework. It was here that she met and fell in love with Charley Crofutt.

Charley and Edith were married in Alliance, Nebraska on July 26, 1916, his 21st birthday. Shortly before their marriage, Charley rode by horseback to take out a homestead. In order to homestead, one had to live and build on the land (which was given away by the government) for five years. At the end of the five years, the individual was allowed to keep the land, if it was improved upon sufficiently.

It was at Lusk, Wyoming that Charley met Herman Hitz, who said he had found a good piece of land about twenty-five miles north of Lusk in the Hat Creek area. Herman offered to ride out with Charley, and so they located the homestead just north of the Hitz's. Charley was impressed with the land, because the grass grew "higher than the horses' bellies" and water was standing in water holes. There was even a lake on the north end of Charley's selected section of land. Later on, our house was built to the southeast of that lake.

Mom and Dad's wedding photograph, July 1916.

CHAPTER 1 – *Our Roots, 1894–1922*

Charley and Edith stayed on at the Spade Ranch, saving what money they could for their move to Wyoming in the spring. Their trip was delayed some by the event of my (Mildred) birth on May 5, 1917. They decided to wait until I was six weeks old, so that my mother and I could fare the journey more easily.

According to my parents, we left Nebraska and started our trek to Niobrara County in June 1917, with all our belongings piled high on the wagon. A small colt trotted beside the team, which Mom was driving, while Dad rode horseback alongside to keep the milk cow moving ahead of us. It was several days' journey from the Sandhills east of Alliance, Nebraska to our new homestead.

Dad, Mom and me, circa 1918.

We camped out each night on our way to the homestead, cooking over a campfire and unrolling our bedroll on the ground near the wagon. Dad and Mom hobbled the horses and turned them loose to graze. One day the chickens got out of the crate, which was sitting at the back of the wagon. Dad scattered some corn and soon had them all back in the crate, and then he fastened it more securely.

When we finally reached the new homestead, Mom and Dad set up the tent they had brought with them. This was to be our home for the rest of the summer. Dad hauled logs from the Seaman Hills about three or four miles southeast of the cabin site for the cabin, shed and corral. Water was hauled in a wooden barrel from Sage Creek, almost a mile to the west.

Hat Creek more accurately describes a country community than a town. Those we called "neighbors" might live several miles away. Hat Creek's boundaries can vary depending upon who is doing the describing. Generally, it includes homesteads and ranches in the vicinity of what was once the Hat Creek Store and Post Office. It is bordered on the south by the chalky limestone hills called the Hat Creek Breaks, which start about 10 miles north of Lusk and run easterly into Nebraska and west all the way to the Converse County line. The northern border is about 15 miles to the north of the Breaks near the George Story homestead. The Black Hills of South Dakota are about 50 miles northeast of our homestead.

In the center of the area, and somewhat to the east are the Seaman Hills that also run east into Nebraska. In fact, the eastern border of the area runs into Nebraska. The headwaters of the Old Woman Creek start about six miles north of Lusk and run north, marking the western edge of the Hat Creek community.

Our homestead, which we always called "the place," was centrally located in the area. About 30 homesteads and ranches dotted the area, although the number was subject to change as families gave up and moved on and as others saw opportunity and moved in. I'm recalling the number from my girlhood.

Families looked and saw open space, almost free for the taking under the

The homestead, 1919.

Homestead Act. In a good year (like 1916 when my father picked out our homestead) the grass could be green and lush into the early summer months. But the area is subject to the whims of nature, and without irrigation, there were many tough years. Winter brings snow and sub-zero temperatures. The winds can be relentless, often blowing the snow generated by large storms. The warmer weather in the summer months could be interrupted by powerful thunderstorms sometimes accompanied by wind, hail and heavy rains. Families tried to scrape out a living, but nature didn't grow much in the area. The only trees were pines on the Hat Creek Breaks and the Seaman Hills with cottonwoods along the creeks. I look back now and wonder how in the world we ever grew watermelons in that gumbo soil on our land.

But there were the people; brave, hard working, giving people, and that is what this book is about – our neighbors and my family. The Hat Creek community was – and still is to this day — a close-knit community, with neighbor helping neighbor.

The center of our tiny community was the post office/general store, about 10 miles south at the site of the old stage station. Andrew and Katie Falconer, who moved from Scotland to Wyoming, operated the store. Mr. Falconer served as our postmaster from 1891 to 1922. The mail came out from Lusk three times a week (and still does to this day). In later years, Dudley Fields, their son-in-law, ran the store. He had married May, Andrew and Katie's daughter.

In the late 1930s, Wilmer Wampler built another store to serve the area. It was located on the north side of Old Woman Creek near Boner Road. John and Geneva Burke later bought this store and moved it near the new Highway 85.

Trips to Lusk were very rare, since almost everything, including groceries, could be purchased from the Montgomery Wards catalog and delivered to the mailbox just three miles from our homestead.

Settling In

Our little family became fairly well settled during the next year. When the U.S. joined World War I in 1918, Dad went back to Nebraska to work in a potash plant to help out with money matters and contribute to the war effort. Aunt Ruth (Dad's sister) came to live with Mom and me while Dad was away.

By 1920, my parents and several neighbors had "proved-up" on their homesteads.

All through the summer and fall of 1918 these two women cared for and harvested the crops, put up the hay, raised a garden, and hauled in the wood for the winter. All while Mom was pregnant with Gerald.

In late fall, a telegram came saying that Dad had caught the flu that was spreading at the time. He was coming back home, arriving back in Lusk by train. Aunt Ruth and Mom hitched the team, stacked some bedding in the back of the wagon, and headed for town. On their way, they dropped me off at the Younkin's, our neighbors. Lloyd Younkin would care for the chores at our place, and Stella Younkin would care for me while Mom and Aunt Ruth were gone.

Dad never returned to the job in Nebraska. He was lucky to have lived. The "Spanish Influenza" epidemic took the lives of more than half a million people in the United States and 21 million people worldwide.

When my parents moved to Wyoming, Chester the colt came with us. He followed his mother as we moved by wagon. Dad broke him to the saddle. We could ride him to bring the milk cows

This is Chester years later with Glenn as the rider.

in from the pasture, and later we rode him to school. He also was a good workhorse and Dad teamed him up with a horse we called Jake to haul wood and do other work around the place.

Gerald and Ihla Faye

On February 19, 1919 Gerald was born at home. I was less than two-years-old at the time and don't remember it. In May of 1920, Ihla Faye was born, but lived only a few hours. She was buried on a small knoll east of the house and a neighbor, the Rev. D. J. Clark presided over the service. Neighbors always helped each other out with whatever chores were at hand. Once, Dad was helping Vern Parker grind grain, with a big stationary engine for power. It had two flywheels that turned all the time, with oil holes. Dad was running the machine, squirting oil in all the right places. It was a cold morning, so he had his gloves on, but one glove caught in a flywheel and pulled his hand over it—just catching his thumb.

Right away they headed for town. Mr. Parker drove his new Model T sedan as fast as it would go, but by the time they reached Lusk, the blood had soaked through a pillow and several bath towels. Dad's thumb was so badly severed that it had to be removed.

Mom, Gerald and I had to stay in town with Dad for several days so the doctor could change the dressings and watch for infection. We stayed in a building with a couple of rooms and a bath. It was the first time Gerald and I

Mom, Uncle Bill and Aunt Ruth (holding me) gathering firewood at Seaman Hills, 1918.

had seen a real bathtub, and it was a treat to bathe in it. It was also special to have an indoor toilet—we had never seen one before.

Social Gatherings

Oftentimes people went to one another's houses just to visit, or play cards. We usually did this on Sundays. One time, Mom and Dad, thinking it was Sunday, went to the Younkin's to visit. Stella Younkin was washing clothes, but she had a pot of beans cooking on the back of the stove. So, she fried some potatoes and made a pan of biscuits. We all ate heartily and had a good visit, with Stella and Lloyd giving Mom and Dad a hard time because it was Monday!

Country-dances were our most common form of entertainment. They were usually held in different homes, with fiddle and guitar or banjo music, and sometimes even a phonograph. The women would take a cake or sandwiches, and there was always a wash boiler of coffee simmering on the stove, and a cardboard box of clean tin cups sitting close by. Us children enjoyed these occasions, playing outdoors until we were tired, and sleeping until daylight when the grownups were ready to go home.

School Christmas programs also drew large crowds. After the "pieces" were spoken and the songs were sung, presents were handed out and a social hour followed. Usually, Santa came with a sack of candy and a popcorn ball for every child, even the smaller ones.

It was an all-day job getting a family ready to go to these affairs. The cake had to be baked and iced, or, if we took sandwiches, the most-often-used meat was chicken. That meant killing, dressing, boiling, grinding, and then mixing the chicken with some form of homemade dressing. Gallons of water had to be carried and heated for baths. The women and older girls curled their hair with a curling iron heated over the kerosene lamp.

As was common in the rural areas of the day, a sewing club was formed in the neighborhood. Meetings were held once a month in the homes of various members. Women came from miles around by team and buggy, brought refreshments and their fancywork, and stayed all day. This was a social event for the ladies. My mother pieced quilts and other practical and necessary items.

PTA meetings were held at the schoolhouse on one Friday afternoon each month. We were dismissed early from our studies and allowed to play outside during the meeting, then we would come back in for refreshments.

For years, on the Fourth of July, a celebration was held in McConnell's Grove, a mile and a half west of our place. Stands were set up where they served soda pop and watermelon; there was even a rodeo. Each family took a picnic lunch, and usually several neighbors set up their food on a tarp stretched out on the ground and then shared the meal together. After the meal, some of the men and older boys played baseball or pitched horseshoes. Meanwhile the women visited and took care of the babies, while the other children played in the creek.

It was in 1920, that Dad and Mom bought their first car—a Model T Ford touring car. The car was open on the sides for nice weather, but had side curtains to be used in the winter. Whenever the top was damaged by wind or hail, new material had to be ordered from the catalog and tacked on to replace the old.

Thus, the homesteaders, like their families before them, had to be able to do things for themselves, such as hewing logs and building their houses and barns, and often times their furniture, replacing the car top, and always making the best of whatever they had.

Dad always half-soled our shoes and sewed them with heavy waxed thread. He was constantly watching for a discarded horse collar or some other heavy and serviceable piece of leather for this purpose. Since no one ever had more than one pair of shoes at one time, each pair had to be polished. This was an advantage to burning pitch wood—there was always soot on the underneath side of the stove lid. We turned these over and rubbed the soot onto the shoes with a rag, and then we polished them to a shine. This made the shoes look nice, but it was hard to keep from smearing the soot onto our stockings, because it kept coming off, even after a good polishing.

Mom's Work

Mom always kept busy at her treadle Singer sewing machine, making all of our clothing except for the boys' overalls, which were ordered, from catalogs. Mom would cut up old coats to make new coats, caps and mittens. She saved

Mom makes sausage while I watch from my highchair.

the scraps to make quilt blocks for warm winter quilts. She salvaged fur collars to line the mittens and insides of earflaps on the caps. We used flour sacks to make dish towels, underwear and countless other things. Later, the sacks came with designs printed on them and we would try to get two or three matching sacks, so we had enough fabric to make a dress.

Mom even had a pattern to make small stockings out of the best of the larger ones. Every summer she would order material to make two dresses for me, and sometimes she would make one for herself. She would also order yards of chambray, enough to make two shirts each for the boys. The fabric was a very pretty blue striped print, which made very handsome shirts for school.

On wash days she had to pack in the water, boil the water, scrub the clothes on a washboard, hang them out to dry and iron them with an iron heated on the stove. She canned food and did all the food preparation, which included killing the livestock. I remember that she did her chores in the morning and her sewing in the afternoon. We also had to take care of gathering eggs, milking the cows twice a day and feeding and caring for the bum (abandoned) lambs and calves. Every evening without fail, the supper dishes were washed, dried, and put away, and the kitchen floor was swept, regardless of anything else that was going on.

Mom always worked so very hard—and she spent a lot of those years pregnant and taking care of babies while taking care of everything else. She had a big garden every year. She processed field corn and beans in a wash boiler, which had to be kept boiling for three hours on the wood stove. We could help snap the beans, but she had to cut the corn off the cob.

Sometimes Mom would work in the fields too. At first she'd cultivate the corn, beans and potatoes. As soon as I could sit on the seat of the corn cultivator and handle the team, I did that. Cultivating took the weeds out from between the rows, but then we'd go through with hoes and get between the plants. She helped with that too. I've known her to hoe weeds in the corn all day and have a baby that night.

To save the peas and corn from her garden, she put these vegetables in clean flour sacks and hung them on the clothesline to dry. Every day we shook them up so they'd dry thoroughly. This usually took several days.

Then there was the mowing, raking, and hauling in the hay. Mom also rendered lard, made her own lye soap and made sausage, pickles, jelly and jam. My parents managed to save enough money to buy a hundred pounds of sugar every fall.

Before frost each year, several neighbors would go out on nearby creeks to pick wild fruit such as chokecherries. They'd usually make several trips. They'd all share the day's pickings when they were done. This fruit made wonderful jelly and jam.

Two More Brothers

Lawrence was born July 5, 1921, out on the homestead. Just 17 months later, on November 30, 1922, Keith was born. Even with the help of a doctor,

Mom almost did not survive his birth. Dad always made sure that a doctor was present for each birth. It was something he did for Mom. I recall that the standard medical practice of the time was that the mother stayed in bed for ten days following each birth.

When labor began, Dad would ride to Frank Hanson's house to phone the doctor. (The Hansons lived four miles west of us.) Years later, Dad and Vern Parker rigged a phone line on the fence between our place and theirs, which was about two miles away. Dad and Mr. Parker followed the fence and soldered every connection. It worked pretty well.

Groceries

Mom and Dad gradually built up their milkcow herd and sold the cream they didn't use. For years, our cream was shipped by rail to Omaha. It was tested for butterfat. The higher the butterfat content, the higher the price we received. Later a creamery was built in Lusk.

We also had a sod chicken-house with two good-sized windows in the south to let in the sunlight. It was warm in winter and cool in summer. Mom had a small incubator that she set up in the house every spring to start her little chickens. She'd set two or three hens at the same time, and then she could put the incubator chicks with them.

The hens laid more eggs than we could use, so we sold the extras at a grocery store in town. Mom also made butter and the store bought it. The money raised from all of these items was used for grocery money.

Dad was embarrassed to be seen carrying a case of eggs down the street, so Mom had to do it. Sometimes, they would drive down the alley and go in the back door of the grocery store. Then, and only then, would he consent to carrying the eggs. He also refused to carry the vinegar jar in for a refill. Vinegar came to the store in a big wooden barrel, and everyone had a bucket or jar for refilling.

My earliest memories of grocery buying would be frustrating today. Customers were not allowed behind the counter. As the customer read off her list, the clerk (usually the owner) would get the item from the shelf, carry it to the counter and add up the bill. There was no choice of brands. It was a real relief when stores put in aisles and let people pick out their own choice of goods.

Bread making took most of a day, the dry yeast cakes worked so slowly. Sometimes we would use a starter, which worked a little faster. Mom always baked several loaves at a time and set them out on the worktable to cool.

Often while the bread was cooling, Mom would go outside to do more chores. Sometimes, when she'd come back in, one of the fresh loaves would have a little hole and all of the insides would be gone. She thought of mice, because we had mice (everybody did), but it didn't look like the work of a mouse. Once she came right back in and there was little Lawrence with his arm inside the bread up to his elbow. He had to stand on his tiptoes to even reach the loaf (he was only two or three years old), and he was eating it as fast as he could. So that mystery was solved!

We also raised lots of dry beans, to share and sell. In the evenings, we cleaned beans that Dad poured on the table. There were hundreds of beans, and we picked through them to take out the sticks, rocks, and bad beans. Then Dad would take the cleaned-up beans to Hat Creek to sell for five dollars for a hundred pounds and trade for anything that we needed.

Dudley Fields ran the store. Dud was a big part of our community. He had all the supplies the homesteaders needed – groceries, clothing, kerosene, hardware and grain and hay for the livestock. When the highway was rebuilt north from Lusk toward Newcastle, he moved the building a mile west to be near it. Later he installed gasoline pumps that were operated by hand. When he was away, he would leave out a gallon of gas in case a neighbor came by and needed enough to make it on into Lusk. Dud always looked after his neighbors.

Sister – Crofutt Family History

Chapter 2
School Years, 1923–1938

In the fall of 1923, I was old enough to start school. Getting to school was the hardest part of starting school.

The nearest school was at Hat Creek about ten miles south of us. Dad bid on and was awarded the bus route from the north. He built a box-type body on the back of his Model T Ford, with benches along the sides for us to sit. We picked up Muriel, Ruth and Vernon Younkin, George and Vera Osborn, Dorothy Myrup, and Bob Scott.

For the first two months of that school year, we went past George Mill's and picked up the two teachers. That was only until their teacherage was ready for them to move into. After dropping us off, Dad continued on and picked up Leslie Roberts and Ed Cook. After the weather turned cold, Les stayed at Cook's during the week.

Morris Himes drove the bus route from the east. During good weather the drivers drove back home. They put a lot of miles on those little Fords. In bad weather they stayed at school in their "buses." The buses had no heaters, but we had little portable kerosene heaters to use as long as the buses were sitting. We all dressed warm—long underwear, long stockings, overshoes, coats, caps, and mittens to keep warm while we were traveling.

Since water was scarce and to keep it from freezing, during cold weather we always drained the radiator into a tub and carried it into the house. (We didn't have antifreeze yet.) One night as we were eating supper, Gerald, who was four, didn't like something on his plate. He was told to eat it, but instead he got down off the bench and backed across the floor. When he came to the tub of water he went right on in, but luckily it had cooled down.

That was a long winter for Mom and Dad. Dad and I would leave for school long before daylight, and return after dark. That left all the chores for Mom to do, along with three little ones to look after.

In the spring when the ice was going out of the creek we couldn't cross it with the car, and there was no bridge. We'd take the team and buggy, pick up the Younkin's, then cross the creek. There we'd leave the team with the buggy and they would eat the hay we had brought for them. We'd fill the radiator and go the rest of the way with the car. At night the procedure was reversed, and we'd leave the car at the creek.

We were always glad for the first day of May, because, by then it was warm enough to go barefoot. Occasionally, we stepped on a rusty nail in a board and had to soak the sore foot in warm Lysol water twice a day to prevent infection. This was before we knew about tetanus shots. Years later, the county health nurse gave free tetanus shots at the school.

Enis
On April 17, 1925, Enis was born. Mom had such a hard time with Keith that she decided to stay in Lusk for the birth. She took little Keith along with her. Mrs. Freeman kept Lawrence and Gerald, ages four and six. When Mom got home, Dad told me to ride home with Bertha Freeman, and pick up Lawrence and Gerald. We mounted the horse with Lawrence and me in the saddle, and Gerald right behind us. We did all right and got home safely, our gentle old horse stopping at fence posts so I could get back on after I opened the gates. I was more accustomed to baby animals than baby brothers, so when I first saw Enis, I asked if his eyes were open yet.

It was this spring that Sadie Hanson came to school one day, and said her folks wanted some of us neighborhood kids—Muriel, Ruth, Vernon, and I, to come home with her and stay overnight to listen to their brand new radio. None of us had ever seen one before. It had earphones we could hold up to our ears and hear all that wonderful talk and music. It was really interesting, but then it got kind of tiresome to seven- and eight-year-old kids. But it was thoughtful of them to ask us.

A few years later, they put speakers on radios and my folks bought one, too. We listened to "hillbilly" music every night and other programs, also. We could get The Grand Old Opry on WSM from Nashville, The Barn Dance on WLS from Chicago, and WHO from Des Moines. There was news and weather in the mornings, and always country-western music.

Dad always said he hoped he had just one kid interested in studying rocks and fossils. (Glenn is, but he never really had a chance to study it.) Dad would spend hours poking and digging around in the badlands where there were lots of fossils and petrified bones.

Once, he found an entire fossil of some animal. He was so proud of that find, that he'd take his friends out there and show it off. One man proved to be a false friend, because the next time Dad went to show it off, all that was left was a large hole where it had once been. The man had stolen it.

Adding On
By this time, 1923 or 1924, Dad added a living room and a bedroom to the cabin. The folks moved their bed into the bedroom. In later years, we had two bunkhouses – one for the boys and one for the girls. For the boys' bunkhouse, Dad sawed pine logs flat on opposite sides and about four inches thick. He notched them on the corners to fit together like a log cabin. They had a wood burning stove and a dresser for their clothes and beds.

Later, Dad got a tar-papered homestead cabin from the Clarks and moved it to our place. He set it up a short ways from the main house. This was for the girls. We, too, had a wood-burning stove, a closet for clothes, and one bed.

In the summertime, it would be too warm to sleep inside, so we'd make up bedrolls and sleep outside. The folks had canvas tarps for that purpose. We usually slept two or three to a bed (quite a contrast to now when each child has to have not only his own bed but also a separate room of his own). We could spread our bedrolls anywhere in the yard. Every night we'd go to sleep to the sound of coyotes howling out in the hills.

The milkcow herd had increased and so had the flock of chickens. With the help of the garden, we always had plenty of food. Dad worked away from home in the summers. He put up hay for neighbors, using his own team and machinery. Later he bought a Fordson tractor and did custom plowing and planting. Still later in the 1930s, he traded for a sawmill. Sometimes he took lumber for pay. He eventually bought a well-drilling outfit.

All this time Mom and us older children milked cows, tended to the crops, put up the hay, and looked after the place. Everybody had a job to do, even the little ones.

Dad and Mom had hand-dug and rocked-up a well up north of the house. We dipped the water out with a bucket on a rope, then carried it to the house in gallon or half-gallon buckets, depending on the size of the kid carrying it. Mom carried a lot of it too, especially on washday. It was easier to get water from the well than out of the creek. But in dry years, the well dried up, so we would have to get water out of the creek.

To get creek water, we had to hook-up the horse to the sled, put the barrel on, and go to the creek a mile away. We had to park up on the bank and carry the water up there in gallon buckets to fill the barrel, because if we filled it down in the creek it would tip off and spill on the way out. So the well was an improvement.

Then Dad traded around and got a well-drilling machine. The first well he drilled was for us. Up to this time we were still hauling water in cream cans or barrels from the creek or from the reservoir. My brothers and I were sure happy when the well was put in, because we were always the ones who hauled the water! This well is still in use today and has some of the best water for miles around.

The county agent had windbreak trees to give out for anyone who wanted to plant them. They were small, maybe a foot high. The folks got enough to plant several rows along the west and north of the buildings. We hauled water from the dam southeast of the house everyday with the four-wheel trailer loaded with fuel barrels. Almost every tree lived and now they make an attractive addition to the place.

Christmas

Every Christmas we always received two small gifts—a toy and something to wear. Usually that meant a little car for the boys, some beads for the girls, and some warm socks or mittens for all. In school we drew names for Christmas. Mom would buy the presents for our classmates without us knowing what she'd purchased. Then she'd wrap them and hide them in a sack. This kept us from telling our classmates ahead of time what they were getting. On the special day, we'd take the sack to the teacher, and she would put the gifts under the tree. Keith always said after the gifts were opened at school we'd go around and see what we'd given our friends.

We always saved the wrapping paper and ribbon—we had to be careful not to tear it or damage it in any way when we opened our gifts. We put it all away very carefully where the mice couldn't get to it. The next year we would get it all out, and piece by piece, lay it on the ironing board to iron out all of the wrinkles. We had to be especially careful not to scorch it.

Birthdays were special, too. We never got any gifts, but always there was a cake. If it was the season of the year when the cows had fresh milk and the hens were laying, we might even have ice cream.

To test the cake to see if it was done baking, we picked a straw out of the broom—always picking the cleanest one of course. Sometimes instead of the cake we had a jellyroll. We always had lots of jelly made from the wild fruit we had picked. Whoever the birthday person was, they got to lick out the bowl the cake was stirred-up in. In later years we shared it with the younger ones. But we learned from the beginning that they were pretty special, so we didn't mind.

Getting to School/Gerald Starts School

By the fall of 1925, the Buena Vista School building was moved closer to our home. Gerald started school that fall, so we both rode one horse. This was Old Dan, the horse that Dad had traded a bull for. Old Dan knew how to fool little kids like us. He didn't like crossing the creek on the ice, even though we'd chop it and rough it up for him. We couldn't even lead him across it. Every morning the folks would watch us go—it was just a little over a mile to the creek. If we didn't come in sight on the other side, one of them would walk down to help us. As soon as one of them came in sight way back up on the bank, Old Dan would walk right across that ice and we would lead him over to a rock and get back on and get to school.

Old Dan would run away every chance he got, but we'd hang on until he got ready to stop. Or if we went to catch him in the pasture he'd just stay out of our reach. I guess he liked to hear us bawl.

Since, it was so far to school, all the parents arranged for us to have a hot lunch at school. Each family took turns furnishing some kind of soup. We carried it in a gallon syrup pail. The teacher would set it on the coal heater at first recess and by noon it would be ready to eat. If there were five families each one would have a certain day of the week to bring the soup. We'd put it in a sack and hang it from the saddle horn. Old Dan didn't like that soup pail bumping along on his side either.

Iris

On May 19, 1926, as Gerald and I were riding home on Old Dan, Mr. Olinger, a neighbor, met us along the way. He told us that we were to go home with him for the night. We were pretty skeptical about doing so without permission from home, but he assured us he had talked to the folks and that was what we were instructed to do.

When we got to the Olinger's house, we found out that Mrs. Olinger was at our house, so Mr. Olinger fixed supper for the school teacher who was boarding there, for his daughter Isabel, himself, and us. The next night we went home from school and found that Iris had been born. Mrs. Olinger was still at our house, helping out.

Getting to School

That fall Lawrence started in the first grade. All three of us rode Old Dan, Lawrence and I in the saddle, and Gerald behind it. Old Dan wasn't in any worse mood with the three of us on him. He would shy at every little thing, especially if a rabbit jumped out from under a sagebrush. But he could never unseat us. We stuck to him like a bunch of cockleburs.

The next fall, Keith started school. Dad traded for a buggy that one horse could pull. I would drive, Gerald would open and shut gates (we had to open three or four gates and cross two creeks to get there), and Lawrence and Keith would ride in the back, out of the wind and cold. We had big flat rocks to put our feet on in the buggy. Every night we'd put the rocks in the oven and by the time breakfast was over the next morning, they would be warm enough to put in the buggy and keep our feet warm on our way to school.

Once in awhile we'd break the shafts out of the buggy. There was a gate at the bottom of one hill—it was always open so we'd get lined up to fit through it. One time the wheel hooked the gatepost and the buggy stopped, but the horse didn't. It scattered kids all over. I had the lines, so I went over the dashboard and the horse dragged me quite far before he stopped. I went back, loaded the lunch pails and coats, Gerald, Lawrence and Keith on the horse and we went home. Dad never did say anything about it. We had to walk for two or three days; then Dad came up with new shafts for the buggy, and we could ride again.

We never could lift the saddle onto the horse, so Dad fixed a rope on a pulley suspended from the rafters in the barn. We could lead the horse under it, hook the rope on the saddle horn, and pull the saddle off. By tying the end of the rope securely to a post, we'd have it ready to go back on. The next morning, we'd just lead the horse under it and lower it onto his back. Then we could cinch it up.

We were too small to reach up to put the harness on the horse. So we figured out how to do it. We'd lead the horse as close to a corral fence as we could, and then Gerald would keep him there while I climbed up with the collar and buckled it on. Then with the harness laced on one of my arms, I'd climb up with it, and put it over on the horse's back. Woe to Gerald if he let him move!

Milking

We always had cats and kittens around the barn and granary to help control mice. We'd pour them a pan of warm milk when we were through milking. They'd gather around and wait, sometimes not so patiently. Once a cat jumped off the fence onto a cow I was milking. She kicked me out through the fence very quickly!

Gerald never liked to milk, so he'd squirt at the cats or anything in sight. One time he squirted it on me—on my arms and legs and in my hair, then he laughed. I took it for awhile, then I went over and kicked his milk stool out from under him. Of course he fell down on the ground with milk spilt all over him. He let out a yell and Dad came out of the garage. He picked up a piece of belting as he came past the junk pile. He saw that Gerald was the one that was hurt. He asked what had happened, and Gerald said I kicked his milk stool. Without hearing my side of the story, he gave me a good belting. After that Gerald would squirt milk on me and laugh. I'd sit with milk running down my skinny arms and legs and just bawl.

We all came to know what it felt like to have the razor strap used on our seats. For years that razor strap served a dual purpose—Dad used a straight razor and it had to be sharpened every time he shaved. It also hung in a handy place in case we misbehaved. One time we went to Frank Potter's house—Frank was a bachelor—and we saw the razor strap hanging from his chair. When Gerald noticed it he asked, "How come Frank has a razor strap? He doesn't have any kids!"

Firewood

For years, Dad hauled firewood from the Seaman Hills, as did most everyone else in the community. The Seaman Hills were important because they were the only nearby source of wood for our community. Soon the wood was gone, and Dad had to haul from the Buck Creek Hills, located northwest of us about twelve or fifteen miles. He'd take the box off the wagon and place the wood directly on the running gears. He'd start by loading the tree trunks on the bottom and fill in all the spaces with pieces of wood until he had it piled higher then the horses' backs. He'd chain it all down and tighten it with boomers.

Going that far required that he leave long before daylight and get home long after dark. We never ate supper until he came home, so Mom would have it waiting on the back of the stove. From time to time one of us, usually me, would go outside and listen for the creaking of the wagon, the jingle of the tugs, and sometimes Dad would be whistling as he walked along the side. The others in the house would be real quiet so I could hear. When he'd come, Gerald, Lawrence, and I would run out and unhitch the team, take them to the barn, unharness them, and turn them out to graze. By that time Dad would be washed and ready to eat and Mom would have dinner on the table.

In the late 1920s, the people of the neighborhood went together and purchased an old store building in Lance Creek. They moved it to a centrally located spot about three miles across the road from us where they could have meetings of all kinds. They named it Pioneer Hall, since it was the first of its kind near there.

On Saturday nights, there was usually a dance, then Sunday school was held the next afternoon. A minister always came out from Lusk to give the sermon. In the winter, when the weather was too cold to have the Sunday school at the Hall, it was held in different homes. Everyone took food for a carry-in lunch.

Pioneer Hall was later moved up by the DeGering turnoff, and even later, Jim Meng bought it and moved it to his place near Red Bird. Today, his son still uses it as a granary.

Lawrence was seven or eight years old, I don't remember how it came about, but he started singing "Stepping in the Light" by himself in front of the congregation. Naturally he made a big hit. Our Sunday school met at Jensen's one time and Lawrence sang his solo. After the service Mr. Anderson gave him a whole package of Black Jack chewing gum. The most we ever got at one time was half a stick, so to have a whole package all to yourself was really great!

Evidently, Gerald saw Lawrence get the gum, because right away they went out behind the house to divide it. Since Gerald was the biggest he thought he should have three sticks and Lawrence two. That sounded reasonable to Lawrence. After all, Gerald was the biggest.

Driving Lessons

Dad showed me how to drive the Model T as soon as I could reach the pedals when I was about 10 years old. One of the first things I did was drive over a bank and break a front spring.

It was some job to change a tire on those cars. The rim was part of the wheel. So it had to be jacked up, the tire pried off the wheel, and the tube pulled out. Everybody carried a can of patching material. The can had a rough place on the lid that you used to rough up around the hole. There was a tube of cement and a good-sized piece of patching material so you could cut out any size or shape you needed. This was adhesive backed with a covering you peeled off just before you stuck it on. Then you pumped the tire up by hand.

Service stations had a machine called a vulcanizer. It put the patch on with heat and it stayed on longer and better. Dad got one from somewhere. It clamped on the tube after the patch was stuck on. There was a basin on the top that you poured some flammable liquid in and touched a match to it. After it burned so long you took it off and your patch stuck tight.

Somehow, Dad had learned to repair cars. He never charged people for this service, although he always seemed to get something in exchange. If a person was stuck with a broken car, they often stayed with us until it was fixed. Dad had an agreement with the high school to use its shop equipment.

Dad was a handy guy. I don't know how he heard about things, but he always made a deal or a trade (like the mill, and the well drilling equipment) and because of this was always able to provide for us.

Lois

On August 20, 1928, Lois was born. Baby care was not an easy task back then. Diapers were made from flour sacks or old blankets. There were no plastic pants—only knitted wool diaper covers. To wash diapers, Mom had to heat water in a boiler and wash the diapers on a washboard with lye soap she'd made. Our "dryer" was a rack behind the wood stove. Mom never had enough milk to nurse her babies, so cow milk was used.

In 1929, Dad traded the Model T for a 1926 Chrysler. I remember going into the garage and admiring how much bigger the Chrysler was. It wasn't any taller but it was longer and wider, and we could all ride much more comfortably in it. There were seven of us children by now.

Schools

The history of our schools is made interesting by the fact that they were designed and built to be moved. Remember, this was before indoor plumbing or electricity. Schools were moved every few years to be nearest the largest student population. Sometimes, the building retained its name; sometimes it was renamed. The following history is as best as I recall it.

In 1924, the Hanson-Anderson School building was moved to a site near Highway 85, and renamed Buena Vista School. Izetta Renswold (Boner) was the teacher that year. There were two ninth grade pupils, Donald Olinger and Sadie Hanson, plus several lower grade students.

Families represented were the Olingers, Hansons, Freemans, Prelles, Younkins, and Crofutts. Some students walked, some came by horseback, and some came by horse and buggy. Teachers for the next three years were Jessie Darling, Elvira Louderback, and Alice Deck. There was no high school.

The building was then moved to a location near Sage Creek, where it was consolidated with the Parker-DeGering School. For four years, ninth and tenth grades were offered here, with Gladys Christian and Alma White serving as teachers. Over the years, teachers for the lower grades were Florence Hanson, Anna Venable, Irma Hargrove, Gordon Hargraves, Marie Mauch, Esther Whitman and myself. The high school teacher was Gladys Christian.

New students joining the school at this time included the Parkers, DeGerings, Hunts, Endicotts and Kapers.

Later, due to a decline in the number of pupils, the building was moved further north on Sage Creek and was consolidated with yet another school. With the addition of the Wampler, Story, Hoffman, Gunn and Maguire children, there were now 31 pupils, with two teachers—Ester DeGering and myself. Four buses were necessary.

After two years parents started sending their children to Lusk on a bus that came out each day. Eventually, it was decided that all the pupils in the district should be bussed to Lusk. By 1946, the Buena Vista School building stood empty and was never used for a school again. Later it was sold, moved, and made a part of the home of Harry and Faye Baker, who had purchased the original Crofutt homestead.

Lyle

On August 13, 1930, Lyle was born. A few weeks later, on September 10, we got home from school, and Mrs. Parker and Mrs. Olinger were there. Mom was lying on the bed. We knew some tragic thing had happened.

The ladies cautioned us to be quiet and to come and see. There was our little baby Lyle on a table in the living room with jars of ice water packed all around him. He'd died that morning.

Mom had bathed Lyle that morning and put him down for his nap. When she checked him later he was dead. So she called the Parkers, and Mr. Parker went down to the Summer's place where Dad was sawing lumber and told him.

Dad went into town and got a little coffin from Earl Peet. The funeral was the next day. Again, our neighbor, the Rev. D.J. Clark held the service. Lyle was buried about a half mile east of the house in the family cemetery. School was dismissed so all the kids could attend.

Harvest Time

Just about everybody raised grain. It was an anxious time, especially those last few days before harvest, watching the sky for the thunder and hailstorms or a heavy beating rain. The grain had to be at the exact stage of ripeness before it could be cut.

Then we went in with a binder, which cut it, tied it in bundles, and kicked the bundles out on the field. Dad operated the tractor, or in earlier days drove a four-horse team, that pulled the binder. At first Mom and I shocked the grain, then, as soon as Gerald could, he and I did. Eventually Lawrence helped, too, and then Keith.

Soon came the big day when the threshing machine came. Mr. Parker had the only one in our neighborhood. He would start at one place, usually his own, and thresh his grain. Neighbors would come for miles around with teams and hay racks to pick the bundles out of the shocks and haul them to the thresher. There they pitched it into one end of the machine. It was pounded out, went through a bunch of screens and fans until finally a stream of grain poured out into a wagon box or trailer along the side and the straw was blown out a pipe onto a stack.

When it was the day for everyone to help at our place, we'd be up at dawn killing and dressing chickens (this was before we had refrigeration), making pies, and preparing vegetables. Usually a woman or two came to each house to help.

We'd put a washpan, soap and plenty of clean towels out by the pump. So then the men could sit right down at the table as soon as they came in without having to wash-up inside. We'd put the food on while they were washing.

Our family always raised a lot of grain, mostly wheat. It was good chicken feed and we would grind it for flour to use along with the store-bought white flour we used for bread and pancakes. We also ground corn for cornmeal.

We had a small mill to grind grain. Dad had rigged a small motor to it. Several neighbors brought their grain to be ground at our place. I remember two families in particular because they were so needful for help—the Cogdills and the Osborns. Scott Cogdill and his family lived three miles north. He was blind, but he had a little son that came with him to show him the way, to help him get through the gates and to drive the team. Walt Osborn and his family lived in a cave five miles south of us. He drove the first team of mules I ever saw. If these folks didn't have grain, Dad would give them some of ours.

Dad made annual trip to Hot Springs to sell our wheat and exchange some of it for flour. The trips were very long and tedious. Hot Springs was in South Dakota, about 65 miles northeast of us. The roads were not paved and were narrow and rough—mostly gravel and dirt. Dad had built a four-wheel trailer from an old car frame, with supports to hold an standard-sized wagon

Helping with the harvest.

box. Gerald and Lawrence had built the wagon-box in high school shop class. He pulled it with our Chrysler.

We would spend days cleaning the wheat, cranking it through the fanning mill to remove weed seeds and any other foreign object. Then we shoveled it into the trailer and tied a canvas tarp over it, fastening it down securely with ropes. Upon arriving at the mill, Dad shoveled the wheat out of the trailer, had it weighed and loaded the flour, and began the long trip home. He'd leave before daylight and get home long after dark. When I was a senior in high school, I went with Dad. On the way home, we stopped at the eye doctor and Dad used money from the wheat to buy me eyeglasses, which I needed very much. Also, by trading the wheat, he'd get enough white flour for the whole winter. It would last a year when mixed with the home-ground flour.

Potatoes

We always planted potatoes on Good Friday. That way we usually had new potatoes and green peas by the Fourth of July. Anyway it was a help to have new potatoes early, because usually the old ones were used up by then. To keep the potatoes from spoiling, we'd sit for hours in the cellar sprouting the potatoes. The sprouts would ruin the potatoes if allowed to grow.

It was quite a job even to cut eyes for planting. Dad rigged an old corn planter to use as a potato planter. He put a long box across the front with a seat at each end. There was a hole to drop the potato eyes through and they'd go into the ground and be covered in a row just like corn. A kid on each seat would feed the eyes through the hole. It worked real neat, too, and was much easier and faster than planting by hand.

Ice

Another community project took place in winter—that of putting up ice. Not everyone took part in this, just mostly the Parkers, DeGerings, Passmores and us. In later years, the Storys did, too.

We had a square icehouse, probably ten or twelve feet wide and eight feet deep, dug out of the ground, with slabs up the sides and poles across the bottom for drainage. Over it all was a roof set on three-foot tall log walls. At one end was a door for entrance and to put the ice through.

When the ice on the dams was eighteen to twenty-four inches thick, the men would gather with their saws and cut it into twenty-four by thirty-six inch blocks, hook their tongs into a chunk and pull it out of the water. Each block weighed about 80 to a 100 pounds. It was then loaded into four-wheel trailers (people didn't have pickups then) and hauled to each family's icehouse to be packed in sawdust. This would insulate it and keep it through the hot summer months. We'd go in and chop off what we needed for iced tea and ice cream. Some people used straw instead of sawdust, but we found that the sawdust insulated the ice and kept it better. Sawdust was plentiful from the sawmill.

Eventually, people got iceboxes and, with a good-sized chunk of ice in one compartment, the milk, butter, and cream would stay cold in the other. There was a pan underneath to catch the water from the melting ice, and you'd better not forget to empty that every day!

Glenn

In 1931, Enis started in the first grade and in 1932 Iris did. That winter, on January 27, 1932, Glenn was born. The weather was bad and the snow was so deep, that it was decided that Mom would stay in town before the birth to be close to a doctor. The Siekerts were good friends and neighbors, so Mrs. Siekert went into town and stayed with Mom.

They stayed at Chris Ruffing's home. The Ruffings had been neighbors to the north of us; but had moved to town to send their kids to high school. Mom was there about a month and Dad stayed at home with us kids. He didn't know how to bake bread, so he made biscuits every night for supper and enough for five school lunches the next day.

Spelling Bee

Every year, starting when I was in the fifth grade, I was in the County Spelling Contest. So for a month or two before the big day, Dad would work with me every night, pronouncing words for me to spell.

The eighth grade was the last year to enter. That year, I went down when I was fourth from the top. I spelled the word right, but it was so easy I spelled it too fast and all the judges said I left out a letter. So, I never made it to the state championship. I'm sure Dad was disappointed, but he never said anything.

Moving Away

That fall of 1932, I was ready for my junior year of high school. We were fortunate that I could attend the country school until then so I could help out at home. Now I had to move to Lusk, because our school only went through tenth grade.

Since it was necessary that I work for my room and board in order to have a place to stay, Mrs. Anstice found me a place with some people by name of Morrison. They managed the IGA Grocery Store there in Lusk and lived in an apartment over the store.

It was very hard for me to adjust to their way of life. I had never been away from home before, had never used any modern conveniences, had never prepared the kind of food they ate. I couldn't understand anyone eating cantaloupe for breakfast instead of pancakes!

After about two weeks, I packed my suitcase and sneaked out one morning right after daylight, without telling them. I don't remember where I left my suitcase while I went to school that day. I didn't have any lunch or breakfast because I didn't have any money.

After school I began looking for somewhere else to stay. I didn't really know anybody or where to start. I knocked on several doors and finally Mrs. Cowger said she usually kept a girl for room and board, but didn't have one yet. She said she'd give me a chance.

They were a different type of people. He had a truck of his own. He hauled goods for people—mostly coal. She helped me with the housework and showed me how. It was much easier for me to get started doing things around there, and much more satisfying.

On weekends, I would go home. Each Friday afternoon, Dad and Chris Myrup, and sometimes Lloyd Younkin took turns picking up the kids from our neighborhood who were boarding in Lusk in order to attend high school. They took us back to Lusk each Sunday afternoon. They never missed a time — no matter what the weather or the road conditions.

May was our junior-senior prom. I guess everybody was excited about it but me. I'd never wanted to go to parties, when I was growing up, even though they had them around the neighborhood. Dad must have thought I wanted to go to those parties—he'd always fill the car with gas and park it at the gate so it would be ready when I was. So I'd go.

For this prom I thought I wouldn't have to go because I didn't have any fancy clothes. But Sadie Hanson gave me a floor length dress and Mrs. Cowger went down to the shoe store and talked them out of a pair of high-heeled shoes for me. They were so uncomfortable I took them home after the prom and never wore them again. Mae Sparks waved my hair. With everybody's efforts I about had to go.

I went over to the room where Edith Parker and the DeGering girls stayed. Milton DeGering and Clyde and Clifford Blackmore came along. Clifford asked if I'd go with him. I didn't really want to, but I did. Edith went with Clyde.

At the prom I made myself as inconspicuous as I could and when the band started to play "Home Sweet Home," I hurried out the door and ran back to Cowger's (taking off my high heeled shoes first). I got my suitcase and was waiting out on the curb when the DeGerings came by to give me a ride home. I should have listened to myself in the first place and stayed home.

Irma

That next spring, on April 18, 1933, Irma was born. Some of the neighbor women helped out and Dad was there to keep the kids in school.

High School Graduation

We had another busy summer and I entered my senior year of high school. Gerald was a freshman. Since, the country high school for grades nine and ten had been discontinued, they'd moved the building north. One building for the Buena Vista Elementary School remained.

In the fall of 1933, I started my senior year of high school in Lusk by staying with Mrs. Penn. My parents took her grain for her chickens and wood for her stove to help pay for my room and board. I graduated in the spring of 1934.

My graduating class, 1934. I'm in the back row, fourth from the right.

After a couple of weeks it was decided that Gerald should be in school, too. The folks came to town and found a room for us to share at the home of the Marvin Wilson family. The Wilsons had previously been our neighbors out north. In this room we had a little kerosene stove to cook on, a table and chairs, and a cot for me. Gerald had a cot in the basement, where he tended the Wilson's furnace.

It must have been shortly before Gerald started school that I was called to the principal's office one day for a phone call. It was Mrs. Anstice, and she said I was to come there right away—she'd arranged it with the principal.

When I got there and saw my parents' car I knew we'd had another tragedy. Mom met me in the hallway and explained that baby Irma had just died in the doctor's office. She had been unable to keep her food down so they had brought her in. She was just five months old. We had the funeral the next day with Rev. D.J. Clark again performing the service. Irma was laid beside Lyle in the family cemetery on our homestead.

Seems like in our younger days Gerald and I had our problems. I suppose I went around with a chip on my shoulder, just daring him to knock it off. He did occasionally, too. But that all changed as we grew up. Gerald and I got along pretty good in our little room and we got to go home every weekend. Needless to say, no one thought I should attend the junior-senior prom this year!

Lola

We had another busy summer, and on August 3, 1934, Lola was born. I was home and old enough to take care of the housework, the baby and the other work.

Shortly after that, Dad started getting ready for me to go to college at Chadron, Nebraska, since it was closest and least costly. Edith Parker had gone to college there the previous winter, so Dad went over there to check on it and to find out how much money it would take.

After he found how much he needed he went to a neighbor and borrowed it. I would need $25 for tuition, $12 for books, and $10 for an activity ticket to attend school functions, some of which were compulsory.

A short while later Dad went to work for Dan Hanson building a barn. Thus he could repay the neighbor and pay some other bills. Then he had enough money for me to register for the other two semesters.

Dad was concerned that we would all have an education. He had only completed the eighth grade, which was pretty good for his day. Had he lived longer he would have given the rest of the kids the chance to go to college.

Mom sewed what she had for me. The others needed school clothes, too. Gerald didn't even go to school that winter. The folks couldn't afford to keep us both in school. By my going then I could get a job and help pay for the rest to go.

Dad built this barn for the Dan Hanson family. Mrs. Hanson is shown with Mom (holding Lola) and Glenn. The barn is still in use today.

Dad took me to Chadron to find a place to work for my room and board. As we went through Crawford we stopped at D.J. Clark's place. They had by now moved to Crawford from north of Hat Creek. Years before, he had been minister of the Methodist Church in Chadron. Dad thought he could show us around Chadron and help us find a place for me to stay, which he did. It was the first time I had been away from home for more than a few days at a time. I didn't get home until Christmas.

We finally found a place for me with the Hartleys, a young couple with two little boys. Mr. Hartley was a teacher at the high school. The five-year-old boy often had convulsions. While I was home for Christmas, he died and they took him back to Iowa for burial. I stayed with their neighbor until they got back.

I was very homesick for awhile, but I was also very busy. Edith Parker stayed in the dorm and her roommate was a girl from the Sandhills named Irene Ostrander. Soon as she found my name was Crofutt she asked if I knew anyone by the name of Bill Crofutt. I said, "Sure, he's my uncle."

Irene had worked on a ranch in Nebraska, with my Uncle Bill. It turned out that the ranch was owned by the Nerns, parents of Faye Baker. Faye's daughter Shirlee eventually married my brother, Glenn. Faye and her husband Harry later bought our homestead and still own it today.

Anyway, Irene said I could go home with her sometime and we'd go see Bill, which I did on Thanksgiving vacation. It was good to get to see him.

A few days before Christmas I received a package from the Montgomery Ward catalog. It was a nice warm coat that some of the Nern family had talked Bill into ordering for me. The coat I had wasn't quite warm enough for the cold weather. I was so proud of the new, warm one.

The next summer I got my first permanent wave. I went to a beauty shop and it cost $1.75. Gerald gave me the money to pay for it; he'd earned it herding sheep for the DeGerings. Each spring after that I went in and had a permanent and took Mom with me. It was a kind of Mother's Day gift to show our appreciation for the hard work she did for us. It wasn't nearly enough, but she was pleased with it.

Teacher

At that time a person could get a certificate to teach in a country school after one year of college. The problem was finding a school that needed a teacher for the coming fall. All the ones in our district had renewed their contracts in March, as they did every year.

I think the first place I went was to Burke's on Indian Creek near the South Dakota border. The man in charge said the Larson-Hales School was open if

I'd be interested. He said there were four pupils. I told him I'd be interested. In just a few days a contract came in the mail—$60 a month. I signed and returned it.

The schoolhouse was a little tarpaper covered building on a ridge midway between Larson's and Hales'. It had no indoor plumbing and the Hales and their wagon delivered water in a cream can.

The school was far enough distance from both places that we rode horseback, except in extremely cold weather, when we walked. Since there was no fence around the school, we put the horses out on pickets. We put the saddles and bridles in a corner of the schoolroom. Along that end of the room we also kept the overshoes, and there were pegs on which to hang coats, caps, and mittens. The coal stove stood in the middle of the floor.

I arranged for room and board at Larson's for which I paid $20 a month. They also furnished me with a horse and saddle. Just before school was out that spring I bought a saddle mare, named Queen, from Larson's. She was a pinto quarter horse. She was four-years-old and quite high-spirited.

Dad and I went to Alliance and bought a saddle. Then I had my own trans-

The author on her horse, Queen, circa 1936.

portation. Even though it was twenty miles home from the schoolhouse to the homestead, I rode it every Friday after school and back on Sunday afternoon, as long as the weather was good. It saved Mom making the trip twice every week.

One of the times Mom was going to drive me, she checked the oil in the car and it was a quart low. She knew to pull the dipstick to check it, but where to put the oil? She asked Glenn, who was just a little guy of three or four. He was sure you just poured it into the dip stick hole. It was really a tedious job but she got it all poured in. She thought he knew—he'd been watching Dad and the boys!

That school year, 1935–36, Gerald went for his sophomore year, and Lawrence started as a freshman. The school district paid $10 a month to the parents for each student that came in from the country. They rented a room upstairs over the Creamery where they could "batch," which meant preparing their own meals and doing their own housework.

Dad managed for a Model T Ford for them to drive to town and back home. They parked it during the week at the place where they stayed. It was open,

The boys are off to the fair. Gerald is driving with Lawrence in passenger seat and Keith and Enis in the back.

Gerald and Glenn, circa 1936.

no top and just a box on the back. One summer they drove it to town for the county fair. They put a seat in the back for Keith and Enis. They drove it for three years.

The next fall Keith started high school too. They had the room over the Creamery again and all three of them stayed there. I went back to the Larson-Hales School—still for the same wages—and paid the same for room and board. They let me keep my horse there without extra charge.

That summer they added six feet to the end of the school building to make room for saddles, bridles, overshoes, and coats. Both years I taught there, we had hot lunches during cold weather. We had a skillet, kettle, and dishes. The Hales would bring antelope steak, or we'd boil rice and raisins, sometimes soup. The Larsons milked cows so we'd take milk. We'd put lunch on the coal heater at first recess and it would be ready by noon.

The following summer, 1937, I went back to Chadron for summer school. At that time they worked two semesters into the twelve weeks. That meant six classes a week in each subject—one day a week you'd go to class twice in the same day for each subject. That kept us busy. Again, I worked for room and board.

I didn't get home again until the end of summer, and when I did I began looking for another teaching job. I was fortunate that they did not yet have a teacher for the Young Woman School (named for the nearby creek). They were paying $80 a month with a $5 raise a month for each of the next two years. Right after school started, I bought a 1931 Model A Ford—a deluxe model in good condition.

In 1937, I bought a portable Underwood typewriter, which saved me a lot of time doing schoolwork, like making tests. Every six weeks, and more often if need be, I gave out tests in each subject. That year for Christmas, Mom and Dad gave me a leather carrying case for getting my papers to and from school. That was a real help in keeping my lesson plans together, and also all the test papers.

Gerald, Lawrence, and Keith were all in high school again. That year they had a room at Lewis Lee's where they "batched," taking food from home. My parents also arranged for them to get any extras they needed at the local IGA Store. They were able to charge items until the end of the month when Dad or Mom would stop by and pay for it. They were always very careful about getting just the necessary things.

Meanwhile the younger ones were going to school and helping out at home. Iris usually helped Mom, while Enis and Lois did the outside chores, usually with Glenn tagging along.

Lois, Lola and Glenn, circa 1937.

Teasing

Lois started the first grade in the 1935-36 year. By the spring of 1938, she entered the county track meet in Lusk, which was held for all the rural schools. She ran in the foot race and came in last. Her brothers really teased her and called here "Speed," but at least she tried.

Iris, too, learned how brothers liked to tease. One time she had a piece of fudge in the palm of her hand. Treats were very scarce around the home. She was thinking how good it was going to taste, when Lawrence went by, grabbed it and ate it. Keith was the only one of the boys that didn't tease them. Usually he took the girls' side in any argument.

Camping in the Black Hills

For several years, before school started in the fall, the folks would take us all to the Black Hills sightseeing. They would get a neighbor to do chores for two or three days. We'd make up three bedrolls, which we tied on the outside of the car, then pack up dishes and food.

One time it was raining when we got there, a steady drizzling rain. We couldn't put bedrolls on the ground, nor could we get a bonfire to burn to cook our supper. We checked into what was then called a "cabin camp"—little log cabins with a "sheepherder" stove for cooking and heating, a box of dry wood, one bed with mattress, a table and two chairs. Water was in a spigot outside and a toilet for everybody to use was out back.

We took in our food and dishes, prepared and ate supper. Our bedding was dry, as it was wrapped in canvas tarps. We made up a couple of beds on the floor for us kids. We thought staying in the cabin was the best part of the trip.

Chapter 3
The Fire, 1938

Every spring, the first part of April, Dad always got a small six-month loan from the bank, to buy tractor fuel and seed for the spring planting. In 1938, near the end of May, the crops were all planted, even the garden, and the incubator was set to hatch the baby chickens we raised every summer. School was out, all the kids were home—Enis, Iris, and Lois from the local country school, Gerald, Lawrence, and Keith from high school—in fact Gerald had just graduated from Lusk High School the week before. I was home from the Young Woman School, where I had taught the past winter. Glenn and Lola were there, too. It looked as if everything was all set for summer. Then tragedy struck!

On the morning of May 24, Mom had gotten up early, as usual, and started a fire in the wood-burning cook stove. It didn't take right off burning so, thinking to hurry it some, she brought in a five-gallon can that was practically empty of kerosene and poured it directly into the stove. We always kept a small can inside in order to pour in just a little at a time. Both parents had cautioned us to always use the small can—never to pour directly from the large one. Evidently the fumes in the empty can ignited and it immediately exploded, throwing flames all over the kitchen and Mom.

She screamed and ran back into the bedroom where Dad was. He beat the flames and smothered them. They started trying to get the window open so they could get out.

The cracks around the window were stuffed with rags and even after he got it open the screen was nailed on solid. He kicked that out and got Mom part way out before he collapsed from the smoke.

The boys were asleep in their bunkhouse and Iris, Lola, and I were asleep in ours. Gerald heard her scream and jumped up. By that time smoke was pouring out all over. He woke the other boys then ran down and called us. Lawrence and Keith were already at the house pulling the folks out.

We got the folks out and knew Lois' bed was just inside another window. We reached in and pulled out all the bedding, even the mattress, but didn't get her.

We put Mom on the mattress and covered her. She was still unconscious, but Dad had regained consciousness. We started looking in the windows for Lois. Gerald said he saw her in there, he was going in after her. I told him not to stay any longer than he could hold his breath or he'd be down too. He went in and felt around but couldn't find her so had to come back out. By that time the flames had the house almost completely covered anyway.

Dad seemed to be rather disoriented—he was just walking around. We didn't know if Mom was even alive, since she hadn't moved yet. I told Gerald to take my car and go get Ray Freeman. Ray was our nearest neighbor. By the time Gerald and Ray came back Mom was conscious.

Glenn remembers standing by Mom, who was now sitting in a rocking chair wrapped in a blanket. She was crying. (Glenn still has that rocking chair.) Ray had a sedan and by taking out the back cushions they could make a bed for her in the back. Ray and I went on to town with her. Dad decided that he was all right.

We went right to the hospital in Lusk. Ray went inside to prepare the staff and Dr. Walter Reckling, our local doctor at that time. I helped Mom out and into the hospital. The flesh was coming loose from her arms and she had other extensive burns.

They immediately put some medication on her arms and bandaged them completely. She went into shock and never regained consciousness. She passed away the following evening about 5:30.

Before they'd gotten Mom all bandaged, Gerald came in with Dad. He'd gotten sick after we left, some from the burns, but most from smoke inhalation. Doc Reckling said to put him right into the other bed in the room with Mom. Glenn recalls, that before Dad came to the hospital, he drove the three little ones (Glenn, Lola and Iris) to Ray Freeman's place. He was excited because he was allowed to shift the gears for Dad. Glenn later realized it was because Dad's hands were burned.

It was still too early in the morning for the telegraph office in Lusk to be open, so we decided we better get back out home. The rest of the kids were still there and did not know what was going on. We stopped at Hat Creek long enough to ask Dud to send telegrams to Mom's relatives, saying that she was not expected to live and that Dad was seriously burned. We gave him their names and addresses. He sent the telegrams, and before night Uncle Paul, Aunt Ocia, Aunt Anna, and Uncle Kenneth were at the hospital.

When we got back out to the place, the entire house structure and contents were nearly burned to the ground. Neighbors were starting to come—some had seen the terrible smoke and others had heard it on the country telephone line when Dud called the telegraph office.

Soon Doc Reckling; Del Shoopman, the county sheriff; and Earl Peet, the county coroner came to investigate and ask some questions. They also searched around in it until they found the ashes where Lois had collapsed and died. She was beside the folks' bed where she'd gone for help. They gathered up some of her ashes and took her with them to be later put in Mom's casket and buried with her.

By noon, women were bringing in food. As soon as it was cool enough, the men started clearing and cleaning up the mess. George Story brought his bulldozer and pickup, and others came with shovels and pitchforks. They hauled it all up in the pasture.

We had a little building by the windmill where we had the milk separator and there was a kerosene stove for cooking or heating water. That's where Mom heated her boiler of water for washing clothes, so the washer was in there too. The ladies shifted things around and set up a long table and chairs that people were starting to bring. It was there that they served meals to the workers.

At first they were mostly cleaning up, then they must have held a meeting of some kind and decided to build another house on the same spot. Right away George was dozing out a basement and others were in there with picks and shovels.

As long as the folks were in the hospital Gerald, Lawrence, Keith, and I stayed in town, mostly with Siekert's. Mom's family did, too. After she had passed away, we were in the hospital to see Dad. He said, "Edith was a wonderful woman. The longer we lived together the better we got along." I think he wanted her family to know that. I never, *at any time*, heard either of them say a cross word to the other.

He also said, "Mildred has always worked hard. She'll take care of things." So it was up to me to carry on. I was proud he trusted me to do it. There wasn't time to plan or organize anything right then. I didn't know he wouldn't live out the day.

He was on oxygen because he had gotten pneumonia from the smoke in his lungs. I guess he knew he was dying. He shook hands all around. For some reason they hadn't let the boys in to see him. We were all in such a daze we just followed what the others said. He died the day after Mom.

Ray and Enid Freeman kept Enis, Iris, Glenn, and Lola during all this difficult time and also during part of the summer until we got settled down again. Iris, just 12- years old at the time of the fire, remembers the horror of realizing they had lost everything—their parents, their sister, their home and all of their belongings.

On May 28, we had a triple funeral at the Congregational Church in Lusk. That morning Dud Fields brought his car to our place for some of us to use for the funeral. People had donated suits for the boys and shoes and other clothing. After the funeral Mrs. Anstice served coffee and cake for anyone who stopped by.

Also, by that time Mrs. Anstice had seen a lawyer, Tom Miller, and arranged for the court to appoint me administratrix of the estate and guardian of the other seven kids, since I was the only one who was of legal age—21. She arranged for us to get $30 a month for Aid to Dependent Children. I didn't cash the checks right away—I saved them back in case we needed it for a doctor or other expense, so they decided we didn't need the assistance and canceled it. We got by anyway.

CHAPTER 3 – *The Fire, 1938*

The Lusk Herald

Vol. 51—No. 51   LUSK, Niobrara County, Wyo.,   Thursday, June 2, 1938

FIRE CLAIMS THIRD VICTIM, CHARLES CROFUTT DIED THURSDAY

The tragedy of last week, in which little Lois Crofutt, 9 was burned to death when the Crofutt ranch home was destroyed by fire and the father and mother terribly burned, resulted in more tragedy when the mother, Edith Mary Crofutt, 43, passed away at the Lusk hospital last Wednesday evening, May 25th from the effects of her burns and the father Charles Crofutt, 42, died the following evening, pneumonia having developed from the effects of inhaling a large quantity of smoke while trying to rescue his wife.

Funeral services for all three victims were conducted from the Congregational church in Lusk on Saturday afternoon, with Rev. Jenkins officiating.

Music was furnished by a quartet composed of Mrs. H. J. Templeton, Mrs. Abdon DeCastro, J. M. Hungate and F. B. Kuns, with Mrs. J. P., Watson presiding at the piano.

The little daughter was buried with her mother and the pall bearers were Dan Hanson, George Story, Lloyd Younkin, John Anstice, Harry Wampler and Albert DeGering.

The pall bearers for Mr. Crofutt were Max Heth, Pat Miller, Ben Seikert, Wilbur Wampler, Albert Olinger and Ray Freeman.

The Peet Mortuary was in charge of the arrangements and burial was made in the Lusk Cemetery.

Complete obituary will be published next week.

* * *

Rebuilding

Meanwhile the neighbors were letting their own work go and working on a house for us. One morning when Mr. Parker came by, Gerald and I were having a dispute. Mr. Parker said they would just quit working on the house right then, if we weren't going to get along. I told him that we would get along.

Then we had a conference—just the eight of us, nobody else. I told them we were all in it together, all of us equal. Nobody was a boss over anybody else. We had to do it ourselves, there was nobody to do it for us, but everybody was going to do his share. We never had any more trouble that I know of.

Later, when I saw Doc Reckling, he said he had offers from several people, some from as far away as Denver, interested in "adopting the younger ones." The word of the fire had been given out on news reports from Denver radio stations. He said he told them, "No one in that family is going to be adopted. They're all going to stay together." I told him, "That's right!" It was better that we all stayed together. Nowadays, news sources often report the reunion of families who have been separated for fifty or more years and are so overjoyed at finding one another. I am glad that we stuck together and did not lose each other after losing our parents and Lois.

Doc Reckling was such a help to me. For years after our parents died, he cared for me and the kids—never charging a dime.

I'd had responsibility for the little ones ever since they started school. I had to get them there and home safely. I never regretted that. I suppose it made me feel rather important. That's the way it was in all the large families—the oldest looked after the others.

My new responsibilities just added on to what I had already done. I didn't think that I was doing any big, brave thing. I took things the way they came. I knew it was just something I had to do. In retrospect, I know a lot of things I could have done better, as does everyone.

Things come easier for people now. Even before the fire, we had to struggle for everything we got. Younger people now can't even imagine what things were like back then. Times were so hard for everyone that the Depression really didn't have an impact on us. I guess things just couldn't get much worse.

Before the fire, I had decided to attend summer school at Laramie. I had

CHAPTER 3 – *The Fire, 1938*

> Lusk, Wyoming, May 25th. 1938
> That we may do what we can to assist the Charles Crofutt family in their great loss, we, the undersigned, subscribe the sums set after our names:

This is just one page from the register listing donations to our family. More than 150 friends and neighbors made contributions on our behalf. We would not have made it without their generous support.

written for all brochures and had even reserved a room at the dorm to stay. For once I was going to school and not have to work for room and board. My highest ambition at that time was to go to Alaska to teach. It was not a state yet, but they needed teachers. I knew a girl in Chadron who was going and I had gotten all the information from her that I could.

Circumstances changed all that but I never regretted it. I had a bigger challenge now. I did notify the college, hoping they'd refund my deposit, but they never did.

By the time school started in the fall, our good, kind neighbors and friends, and even strangers, had our new house ready for us. The house had two bedrooms, a full basement, and wall-to-wall linoleum. We were given all the furniture, clothing, dishes and bedding we needed.

People left their own work undone to help our family in our greatest time of need. Petitions were circulated in nearby towns asking for donations. Some donors signed their names, some simply signed, "A. Friend." In those hard times, each donation was from the heart, and often, from the bottom of the donor's pocket. These donations of time and money were so greatly appreciated. Even now, sixty years later, we are all thankful for the good people who helped us.

Chapter 4
Carrying On, 1938–1941

The local paper reported:

> *The children will carry on at the farmstead, with the oldest daughter, Miss Mildred, accepting the leadership of the group. This splendid attitude of holding together a family so sorrowfully stricken, has earned and received the commendation of a multitude of persons, with an added hope that the future may bring to each of them a satisfaction and degree of happiness which may help alleviate the great sorrow that now burdens them.*

We were now a family of seven. I had turned 21 just three weeks before the fire. Gerald was 19, Lawrence, almost 17, Keith, 15, Enis, 13, Iris, 12, Glenn, 6, and little Lola was not quite 4.

Lola was too young for school, so whenever Gerald was home, she stayed with him. Otherwise she stayed with Margaret Chard during the week, while I taught school.

Lawrence was a senior in high school and Keith was a junior. They had a room in town and "batched it." Lawrence had a Model A Ford, so they had a way to get home on weekends. Lawrence had enough credits by mid-term to earn his diploma, so he left school early and went up by Powder River west of Casper and worked on a sheep ranch. We always made sure Keith had a ride home on weekends.

Everybody had his share of work to do. One of Glenn and Lola's jobs was to bring in wood and chips for the fires. The wood was sawed and split, ready to bring in, but they would split the kindling. They usually did this right after school.

One night it got dark and the woodbox was still empty. They were reminded that they hadn't done their chores yet. They took the flashlight outside; it always seemed to need new batteries, but it gave them a small circle of light. Soon Lola came back in crying, with blood dripping off the top of her head. She said Glenn hit her over the head with the axe.

It turned out not to be that drastic. They were not too brave about being out after dark and she had crowded in too close to where he was cutting. He

Glenn and Lola, circa 1940.

must have only bumped her because it was a small cut. We soon stopped the bleeding and cleaned it up. After that they always made sure that they had their wood in before dark!

Lola had a little toy iron that she used for her doll clothes. She had a special place near the bottom of the wood heater where it just fit, but she was afraid to test it to see if it was warm. One time, she asked me to test it, but I was busy and ignored her. She set it on my arm. Well, she got my attention and it was hot! She went on with her ironing as usual.

We had relatives living on the Pine Ridge Indian Reservation in South Dakota—Grandma and Grandpa Crofutt and some of their families. Uncle Ott and Aunt Grace Crofutt had a place with more grass than they needed for their stock. They suggested that we bring our cattle there to pasture. It was about 90 miles from us.

Gerald was sure he could trail them across there. He did, riding Queen, heading straight east from home. I don't remember his taking any food or bed, just a blanket to spread on the ground. He planned to stop at farms and ranches along the way, which is what he did. But as I look back on it now, I realize those places were few and far between.

It must have taken him a week or more, but finally a neighbor of Ott's brought him home to save him the long ride back. The man had a pickup with a stock rack so he brought Queen home too. After about a year, Ott couldn't keep our cattle any longer, but instead of having Gerald come back to trail them home, they had another neighbor truck them back to us.

Harry and Bertha Wampler were neighbors about three miles west of us kept the cattle for awhile. After Enis went to work at Storys he took them there. I had the Wampler's son, Ernie, as a student.

We had sheep, too. For years the DeGerings and Boners gave their bum lambs to us. With them and their increase the folks had quite a herd of sheep. The Wamplers pastured them with their sheep for awhile, but eventually we sold them to the DeGerings.

The sheep remind me of a plant we called lambs' quarters—it was like spinach. It grew as weeds all over the place. The best ones grew in the sheep pen, which we no longer used for sheep. Even though we always washed them thoroughly Dad would never eat any.

Mom's incubator had been set up in the house at the time of her death, so it was destroyed in the fire. After that we bought chicks every spring from a hatchery in Lingle. I remember back then, people ordered chicks through the mail. When you'd go into the post office you could hear them peeping. It was quite an exasperating time for the postal employees.

Gerald and Lawrence always managed for the winter's firewood. One fall they went down to Lue Osborn's near Hat Creek for it. They'd cut it down and saw it up during the week, then we'd all go with the trailer on weekends to haul it home.

They always carried a lunch when cutting wood, as we did going to school. I remember one incident that came up at that time. We had lettuce for sandwiches and nothing else except bread and possibly butter. In order to make them taste a little better I sprinkled salt and pepper on the lettuce. When they came home that night they were laughing about their "salt and pepper" sandwiches. They never missed a chance to tease.

1939

That summer the school building was moved again. This time it was moved out by Boner Road, near the Old Woman Creek Bridge. The Pine Valley school building was moved near there to again form a consolidated school, with all eight grades, thirty-one students, four bus drivers, and two teachers. Esther DeGering taught the first four grades, I taught the four upper grades.

For years the State of Wyoming gave achievement tests on each subject at the end of every school year. The tests were sent to the teachers, and the teacher in turn was required to ask two parents to be present as the envelopes were unsealed and the tests were distributed. The testing lasted two days. Later the results were mailed out to each student, along with the notice as to whether (or not) they were promoted to the next grade. This practice has long since been discontinued.

Ernie Wampler, one of my students recalls:

"In 1939 my new teacher was Mildred Crofutt. When I think about Mildred, I think about the loss of her parents and a sister in the fire that consumed their house. There followed a great outpouring of sympathy, and the community built a new home for Mildred and her siblings. Mildred was able to lead her brothers and sisters into adulthood.

"That country school was not easy for Mildred. She had to come each morning to a frame building with no insulation, no electricity, and a coal-burning heat stove. On cold days, it hardly got warm before the bus came to take us home again. Another rural teacher told me that when the school did warm up, the smell could get to you, as bathing was not routine in the winter back then. I remember one winter when I was trapping skunks to raise money. I must have smelled pretty bad, as Mildred suggested that I lay off skunk trapping!

"About twice a year, the county Superintendent of Schools, Mr. Kuns, would come to check us out. Sometimes he brought a movie projector that ran on a pack of batteries that he carried in the trunk of his car. We would cover all the windows and he would show educational movies. It wasn't like the movies in town, but it was good anyway.

"Mildred was a very kind and patient person, doing her very best under trying circumstances."

Seven of my students and me in front of Young Woman School, circa 1938.

That fall, 1939, Keith was a senior in high school and Enis was a freshman. I arranged for their room and board at the Matthewsons, who lived a mile southeast of town. Mrs. Matthewson agreed to keep Keith and Enis for the $10 each the district was paying. They walked in to school from there.

With eight grades and thirty-one pupils, we had a much better Christmas program. That year we had it in the Community Hall, across the road. Neither school building was large enough to accommodate all the parents.

Almost from the beginning of each school year my students became excited about the Christmas program. They enjoyed inviting and entertaining their parents and neighbors. Each student memorized a "piece" to recite, and we had little plays.

We had no musical accompaniment for songs, but the students all lined up and sang, usually "Jingle Bells" first. That got the little ones interested, then they sang "Star of the East" and finished with "Silent Night." On "Silent Night," I always told them to sing out until the last verse, then lower their voices and sing it softly. They did, and it would be so quiet in the room for two or three seconds, then the audience would really applaud. Gifts were distributed, candy and nuts, too, while the grownups visited.

I remember one Christmas program in particular. I was a little girl, too young for school. Dad's brothers Frank and Otto were visiting us. Dad took us in a horse-drawn sled while his two brothers rode horseback. Otto had been asked to be Santa. He asked the pupils, even the little ones, if they'd been good. Gerald, who was about three, said "Hello, Otto," real loud. Mom tired to stop him, but Gerald knew who it was. When Santa left, Gerald hollered, "Goodbye, Ott." Mom was really embarrassed. I remember that year because Mom's younger sister Hazel lived with us that winter and was in the Christmas program. We went to the program to see her since none of us were in school yet.

The pupils had drawn names for a gift exchange, so there was a gift for each student from a classmate, plus one from the teacher.

One year, when I was teaching, after we got home from the program, Glenn, who was in the second grade, started crying. He said, "Look at all the things you got and look what we got." It was true! I had a gift from each family and they had two little gifts—one from the teacher and other from the pupil who had their name. Right then, I would gladly have given up all I had, if only my gifts could have been used by the younger kids.

By now, Lawrence and Gerald were both working away from home. Usually I took the car to school on Friday morning and went on in to town to bring Keith and Enis home. Likewise, I usually took them back early on Monday morning and went on down to school in time to start at 9:00.

One spring morning we were headed to town. We'd stopped at the Hat Creek Store—Dud was always open early. As we turned back onto the highway a string of cars was coming from the south. They were not signalling that they were going to turn off, and there was plenty of room anyway. Just as I got turned, the first one hit our left rear fender. Knowing I had to get on to town and back out to school, I kept on going. I told Keith it felt like something was dragging. We pulled off the road and checked. The fender was rubbing on the tire. We both braced our feet and pulled it out.

About then the fellow who ran into us came alongside and said we better come back to the store. We did and I showed Dud that it was that guy's front fender and our rear one that was damaged. So how could it be my fault? He agreed and said to go on, he'd take care of it. We never did hear any more about it. I don't know what that neighborhood would have done without Dudley Fields—he helped us all in so many ways.

1940

In 1940, I decided I should go back to summer school. By this time they didn't crowd two semesters into a summer, so it lasted only nine weeks instead of 12. I went back to Chadron because it cost less. I got room and board for $25 a month. I went home every Friday afternoon and back every Monday morning. One Friday, I had a flat tire on the overpass at Van Tassell. The road sign definitely said "No Parking on this Overpass." I pulled over as close to the guardrail as I could and changed the tire.

When I got to the Independent Refinery in Lusk where we traded, Bill Hitz said those rear tires should be replaced with new ones. The next Friday I had him do just that.

Part of the time while I was gone, Lawrence, now age 19, was home with the younger ones. When he was going to be gone he'd take them to Chard's to stay during the week. Iris was 14, Glenn was eight and Lola was just six.

Enis, 15, was now working at the Storys and coming home weekends on horseback.

George and Freda Story were so helpful to the family after the fire. George was the one who started rebuilding our house. Enis worked for them for over 16 years and they treated him like a son. Freda Story shared this recollection of our family:

> "I never had the privilege of knowing Charley and Edith Crofutt very well. I became acquainted with the children after the fire. Keith worked for us after finishing school before going into the Army. He had such a sweet nature. I remember him being so gentle with my daughter, Amy, who was just a baby at that time. He wanted me to teach him how to crochet so if he ended up being wounded in combat and in the hospital he would have something to do.
>
> "Enis came to work for us after he finished school and stayed with us for 16 years. I think Enis started the "Big Brother" program. His was really a big brother to my son Rex and to our other children. He was certainly a part of our family.
>
> "The children always called Mildred "Sister" (and I notice they still do). They had had a good training and helped her out a lot. I feel fortunate to have known this family."

Keith, 18, must have been working at the Clark's and he bought Alan Clark's pickup truck. Gerald was now 21 and was drilling wells with Dad's well drilling outfit. Anyway, we were all home Saturday night and Sunday.

I sewed dresses for Iris, Lola and myself, but ordered the boys' clothes ready-made from the catalog. One time Lawrence needed a shirt. I don't remember why I was going to order only one shirt, but maybe there was only money for

one, and he was the neediest one right then.

I found one in a catalog, but this catalog didn't list sizes like catalogs do now. I read it and understood that we needed to measure from the middle of the collarbone. He was ticklish so we weren't making much headway until someone checked the catalog again and found it should be measured from the middle of the collar-band, not the collarbone!

It seems that the boys each had his own shirts and overalls, but they all wore the same size underwear and socks. Whenever Iris or I washed those we'd put them all together in a drawer in the bedroom. As soon as each one got home Saturday afternoon, the first thing he did was to go in, pick out the best looking underwear and socks, and hide them. Then he'd bring in water for bathing and get it to heating.

Somebody gave Lola a squirt gun. Lawrence would wait until Keith or Enis were in the tub. He'd fill the gun with cold water, open the door a crack, and squirt them just to hear them holler—'course they always did. I finally got the thing and hid it from him.

Iris smiles for my camera, circa 1940.

We always went to town on Saturday night. It was about the only recreation we had. We bought our groceries, the younger ones went to the show or played bingo and the older ones went dancing. Sometimes Keith or Enis preferred to stay home with Glenn and Lola.

In the spring when it was muddy, sometimes I needed to go to town on Saturday morning for school supplies or something. If I needed chains on the tires to get to the highway, Lawrence would follow me that far and take them off. He'd tell me that when I came back, to turn off the highway and he'd be watching to come back over and put the chains back on. I would have to wait only a little while and I'd see him coming. Probably they had all been watching.

In the fall of 1940, Lola started the first grade and Iris was a high school freshman. Iris stayed with the Deetjens. Enis, who was a sophomore, "batched" with Dean Leimser at the Wyoming Cabin Camp. The "camp," was a motel with individual cabins, a common toilet and no shower.

During these years, Gerald mostly worked at the Clark's, but he did drill some wells too. He bought an old Ford truck for $25 so he could pull the rig. It also would haul his fuel and water barrels and other necessary equipment.

Lawrence operated a "cat" building dams—part of the time for Jim Pfister and later for Ed Hales. During the winters he was mostly home. Then he operated haying equipment for Ed.

Keith worked awhile for Ray Larson, but when he wouldn't milk the cows before breakfast, Ray brought him home. He did work for Alan Clark for awhile after Gerald went into the Air Corps, then for Dan Hanson.

After the fire I was glad I had a job that would support us. The school district was considerate to give me a choice of schools. They held back thirty dollars a month for the nine months in order to encourage teachers to go to summer school, but they added it all to the final check in May. That helped to get us through the summers.

Before school started every fall we started getting clothes ready. That was even before the fire. We'd get the Montgomery Wards catalog out, open it to the shoe pages, and find the chart that was always there so that by using it we could tell what size each one needed. There was a diagram there the shape of a footprint with numbers on it. We could step on that print and by careful measurement it would show what size to order. If by chance they didn't quite fit when we got them we could package them back up and return them for the right size. The catalog company always refunded the postage on anything returned to them.

It seemed like shoes were the biggest expense in clothing us. I don't know how our parents ever managed, but we all had new shoes to wear the first day of school. The catalog always had colored pages of material too, and that helped us to decide which we wanted for dresses.

Sister – Crofutt Family History

Chapter 5
The War Years, 1941–1945

During the school year of 1941–42, Iris had an apartment at the Myrup's. Enis batched with Mike Burke in an apartment at Lewis Lee's. He and George Bryant were the same age, having both been born on the same day. They were almost inseparable all through high school. Iris always seemed to be their special target for pranks.

By this time we had replaced the wood-burning heater in our house with an oil heater. We also had gotten a 32-volt windcharger, and some appliances to go with it—a motor for the washer, a radio, and an iron for ironing clothes, plus lights in every room. The boys had put a barrel by the windmill and piped water into the house, installed a sink and set up a pitcher pump. These all made work easier, which helped, since most of us were working away from home.

On the morning of December 7, 1941, I turned on the radio to KLZ in Denver, as I did every morning, and right away all the news was about the bombing of Pearl Harbor. I hurried to wake Gerald up and we wondered what could happen next, but we knew that our country couldn't let Japan get away with that. All the boys around the neighborhood wanted to go serve our county.

On January 1, 1942, Gerald and Vernon Younkin went to Cheyenne to register for the Air Force. They assumed by volunteering early they would get into the branch of service they wanted. They were taken immediately into training, and were then stationed at different forts around the country. They were separated because the service seldom let friends or brothers serve together. Gerald served in the Army Air Force.

Gerald kept in touch, writing letters home every few days, and always making sure we had his new address. We always treasured these letters, and we now have them in an album so that we can reread them and remember the concern we felt for him. We also wrote him every few days and he also treasured these letters, especially the ones from Lola, Glenn, Iris, and Enis. Oh yes, they wrote faithfully, too. He kept all our letters, and he had bundles of them when he came home.

> *Jan. 24, 1942, Sheppard Field, Texas – Dear Folks, I'm still in the Army and have been for 16 days and haven't got used to it yet and I don't suppose I ever will. I signed up for the duration of the war and 6 months after it's over.*
> *Good Luck, Gerald*

Shortly after Christmas, in early 1942, we all, one after another, came down with measles. Lawrence brought Enis and Iris home from school in town and they both had it. A day or two later, Lawrence had it, too. Freda Story, Bertha Wampler, and Mrs. DeGering took turns staying with us twenty-four hours a day. They brought food and prepared meals. Harry Wampler did the chores and milked the cows. When we got to feeling better, we wrote to Gerald and two or three weeks after he got the letter he had measles!

> *March 29, 1942, Barksdale Field, LA. – Dear Folks, Well, that old measles bug bit me. I broke out with the measles Thursday morning, so I'm in the hospital now. I'm still pretty sick, but am getting better. I suppose I'll be in here for nearly a month. I was supposed to go to Florida today. I don't know what they will do with me when I get out.*
> *Good Luck, Gerald*

During his measles, Gerald's outfit was packed and moved. Gerald was left behind in the infirmary with no supplies—his war bag had gone on with the rest. Luckily, his outfit was delayed, so he was able to join them.

CHAPTER 5 – *The War Years, 1941–1945*

In April, he wrote us from his new address.

> *April 13, 1942, Fort Myers, Florida – Dear Folks, Well I finally got settled again, for the present anyway. I came down from Barksdale on the train alone, so I had a pretty fair time. It's the first real freedom I've had since joining the Army. It only lasted 3 days.*
>
> *I am stationed about 10 miles out of Ft. Myers, right out in the wilderness. It's a regular jungle. The country is full of snakes and mosquitoes, and that is about all. These mosquitoes that fly around the swamps are nearly as big as a plane. When they sit down and start grazing on a guy it's about the same as getting stuck with a pitchfork. It sure is hot and sultry down here in the daytime, but it gets kind of cold at night. I sure don't like this place.*

In reviewing Gerald's and Keith's letters all these years later, this is one of the very few with any complaining (except about the weather). But he went on to describe his trip to Florida and the sites:

> *I sure saw a lot of sites I'd never seen before, as I was coming down. I saw the ocean for the first time in my life. I saw some ships in the dry docks at Mobile that had been torpedoed. It looks funny to see a body of water that extends so far. It looks like it just goes out of sight over a hill. There are some really pretty places down here, but I would rather be up north where it isn't so hot.*
> *Good Luck, Gerald*

During the 1942-43 school year, Enis was a senior in high school and Iris was a junior. They both stayed with Margaret Chard. Glenn, Lola, and I were still going to the school north of home. We rode Mr. Younkin's bus.

CHAPTER 5 – *The War Years, 1941–1945*

That summer, Gerald tried to become a pilot in the Army. He had his heart set on it. This is what he wrote home:

June 26, 1942, Lakeland Florida – Dear Folks, I took a physical exam yesterday morning for glider pilot, but couldn't pass it. My blood pressure is too high. The doc. was good about it. He tried every way he knew to get it lower, but it wouldn't come down enough to for me to qualify. That means that I'll never be able to pilot any kind of an Army plane. If we go north for a while before we go across I'm going to try it again. I think it's this hot climate that caused all my trouble. I'll sure be glad to get out of this hellhole of a state.

I sure hate it because I couldn't make the grade. I had my sights set pretty high on becoming a pilot of some kind. It's no one's fault, though. It's just one of those things.
Good Luck, Gerald

The next month, Gerald wrote us again about his hopes.

August 17, 1942, Harding Field, LA – Dear Folks, I am going to take an examination physical in the morning for aerial gunner. I am sure hoping I can make the grade. I've tried so many things and failed, so I guess I can stand it again.

It does look like Keith will have to disappoint a lot of women, and join the Army doesn't it. Well, I hope he gets into something about half-decent anyway.

I made out an allotment today from my pay. From the first of November on, you will be getting $20 a month, not much money, but it may help. You can use it to pay off my debts and for anything else you want. If there is any left over, put it in the bank, so you can draw it out in case I don't get back. That way, you see, I'll have a little money *saved up, when I get back. $30 is plenty for me to spend, and besides we get a 20% increase in pay when we get across.*

Good Luck, Gerald

In October 1942, we got a telegram from Gerald that he was to be on leave in Cheyenne by bus on a certain date. Lawrence and Keith went there to pick him up. During that day George Story came to the schoolhouse with another telegram telling Gerald to report back for duty in three days. We tracked down the boys by telegram, telling them to hurry home.

October 1942—We all enjoyed Gerald's visit while he was home on leave. It was the last time we were all together.

We knew he'd have to go right back without having any time at home. Before school was out that night, George was back with money enough for plane fare, so Gerald could have extra time at home. George had contacted neighbors and they had donated enough money for the ticket. Alan Clark volunteered to drive Gerald to Denver to catch the plane. They had even arranged for school to be dismissed those three days so we could all be home together and so I could go to Denver with him too.

We'd never have made it out there without the help and encouragement of all the neighbors. They helped us through everyday life and through every crisis that came up.

Christmas 1942 was our first Christmas without Gerald. On Christmas Eve he wrote us.

> *December 24, 1942, Camp Kilmer, N.J. – Dear Folks,*
> *Decided to write you so you would know I'm still alive and kicking. I'm fine myself. Hope you all are the same. I am still in New Jersey. Probably will be until after New Years.*
>
> *I heard that there were rumors going around up there to the effect that a ship I was on was sunk and I was one of the missing. You don't want to pay any attention to things like that. You will be officially notified by the Gov. if such a thing should happen, but it won't. I hope.*
>
> *Well, tonight is Christmas Eve. I can just see your house, with the Christmas tree in the corner by the east window. I can see you and Iris trying to keep all the boys out of the candy and nuts and away from the tree decorations. I am going to miss it all a lot. We have a tree in our barracks. It looks kind of lonely though.*
>
> *Good Luck, Gerald*

Enis graduated from Lusk High School in 1943. He went to work for George Story, where he stayed for 16 years. During the War the Storys had pastured the cattle from our estate. Also Enis got a FHA loan and bought cattle. George

John and Mildred's wedding photograph, March 1944.

let him run his cattle along with the Storys' cattle.

In March 1944, I married John Bryant in Gering, Nebraska. His family was from our "neighborhood" — they lived near Hat Creek. Our son George was born the following March. That fall, George had a very serious mastoid operation. He also contracted whooping cough, so we moved to Lusk to be near the doctor. John went to Denver to look for work. Lola stayed with me in town, Glenn stayed at the Hales' to remain in the country school.

During the summer of 1944, Lawrence married my husband's sister Tiny, in Gering.

Keith

In April of 1943, Keith asked the draft board to draw his name for military service. Sometime before that he had tried to get into the Navy, but he had a heart murmur, so the Navy wouldn't take him.

Keith was working for Dan Hanson. Boys who were doing farm or ranch work could get a deferment, since they were needed to produce the food for the military and for the civilian population. Dan and his mother came over to see if I would have Keith deferred. (Evidently they didn't know he had volunteered.) They said they would gladly sign papers to keep him. I said it was up to Keith. Most of the other boys his age were going. Since then, I've wondered lots of times if I did right in not keeping him home.

Keith passed his physical and was soon called into the Army. He took all his training at Fort Riley, Kansas in the cavalry. In June he wrote us.

June 24, 1943, Fort Riley, Kansas – Dear Folks, I got your letter today and was I pleased. A letter from home sure brightens things up for a feller. It gets so lonesome and monotonous that a guy gets disappointed with everything in general.

CHAPTER 5 – *The War Years, 1941–1945*

> *They moved everybody that was over five foot ten to different barracks so there wouldn't be different sized guys in each platoon. I don't know what difference it makes, but I guess it is some screwy idea the Army has. I sure hate it too. Most of the guys that were in my barracks were from Colo. and Wyo. and were easier to get along with. The place I am now in are all Easterners and Southerners and are hard to understand and are more ready to get mad at a guy for nothing. I guess maybe I will get used to them.*
>
> *Love, Keith*

Keith came home in the fall for a two-week leave. Gasoline rationing was so tight by then, even for country folks, that he did most of his visiting by horseback. But he did get around and see most of the neighbors. We didn't know that was the last time we would ever see him. Keith also had a girlfriend, Ruth Clark. They were planning to be married after the war. Ruth was the daughter of Alan Clark and the granddaughter of the Rev. Clark.

On the War front, Keith was shipped out to the South Pacific. He had training in Australia; then they advanced to New Guinea and the Admiralty Islands. That was our first Christmas without Keith and his last. He wrote us on Christmas Day.

> *Dec. 25, 1943, Somewhere in Australia – Dear Folks, I received your long waited for letter yesterday. I sure was glad to hear from you.*
>
> *Here it is Christmas Day. It doesn't seem much like Xmas, it seems more like the Fourth of July. It's warm and sultry. Just opposite of the temperature of that I am used to up there. I am not celebrating as much as I probably would be doing if I were there. I will make up for lost time though probably if and when I get back there.*
>
> *Good luck and a very happy New Year to you all.*
>
> *Love, Keith*

Christmas continued in April for Keith when he wrote home about receiving his gifts.

> *Admiralties Is., April 13, 1944 – Dear Folks, How are you all making out these days? I suppose spring is in the air with green grass everywhere?*
>
> *I finally got the Xmas package you sent. It was sure long enough getting here, but I sure was glad to get it. The pen & pencil set is just what the doctor ordered. I can use everything that was in it. I will never forget it.*
>
> *It sure is hot over here, a fellow sweats continually. It has been this way since I have crossed to the South of the Equator. I will sure be glad to get back to a high and dry climate like good old Wyo.*
>
> *Everything is going all right with me. I am in no danger. Have you been hearing from Gerald very often?*
>
> *I have to go to work, so will close. Write often.*
>
> *Love, Keith*

By this time, Gerald was in Africa, then Italy and wrote us as often as he could. After a look at reality, he was glad Lawrence and Enis were still at home.

> *Italy, July 5, 1944 – Dear Folks, This will probably cause you all to fall over in a faint, getting three letters from me in ten days. Hope this finds you all well. I'm doing well myself.*
>
> *I received your package day before yesterday. Sure was glad to get it too. You helped my morale and about nine other boys that live in the same tent. I never really cared much for candy until I got over here, now I'm plum nuts about it. I guess that's because it's so hard to get.*
>
> *I don't worry very much about how things are being taken care of at home. I was mighty glad that Lawrence and Enis were rejected from the Army. They can do so much*

CHAPTER 5 – *The War Years, 1941–1945*

more good at home. I know that John is doing his best to keep the ball a rolling. He is just as capable of taking care of the place as any of us boys and no doubt is more dependable, as he has a future to look forward to while we just looked forward to the next day. I don't think I'll ever settle down around home any place. I haven't really given much thought to the future. I'm not young anymore, by a long ways. Two more years like the last two and I'll be ready for the Old Soldiers Home.

Well, I'll bring this thing to a close. Write when you can. I'll do the same.

Good luck, Gerald

Both Gerald and Keith went out of their way to assure us that they were never in any danger, but sometimes a line or two would slip through and we'd wonder what had happened. We received one such letter from Gerald.

Italy, Aug. 22, 1944 – Dear Folks, I'm sorry I didn't write sooner, but it just couldn't be done. I spent three days in France, but I'm back in Italy again now. I'm in a hospital, nothing serious though. Expect to get out in a few days.

I've been away from my outfit since around the first of July so haven't had any mail during that time. I'm sure anxious to catch up with my outfit for that reason. A fellow gets to feeling uneasy about things at home when he doesn't get any kind of news at all. Of course, it's absolutely no one's fault. It's just one of those things.

Well, I can't think of a thing to write, so I may as well bring this thing to a close. I'll settle down and write a good letter in a couple of days. You will have to excuse this pencil, as I lost my pen in the last little fracas I was in. Write when you can. I'll do the same.

Good luck, Gerald

On October 20, 1944, Keith's outfit — the 1st Cavalry Division, invaded Leyte in the Philippines. He wrote us his last letter on September 29. We didn't get it for a long time. We were a little worried about not hearing from him. Our main source of news was the news clips, which were shown before the movies and a little information on the radio.

> *Admiralty Isles, Sept. 29, 1944 – Dear Mildred and John, I got a letter from you tonight, not a very long one, but still a letter which I am glad to get. I am fine.*
>
> *I could sure go for some of that cool weather that you mentioned. I would probably freeze in some of the warmest weather up there though after being here for so long. I am almost getting used to the heat now…*
>
> *That sounds pretty good the price of your lambs, calves must be pretty good money too, aren't they?*
>
> *When you write let me know what ever you know of Gerald. I never hear from him.*
>
> *I haven't much more to write, so until next time, so long. Write.*
>
> *Love, Keith*

Gerald was worried, too and wrote us.

> *Italy, Jan. 8, 1945 – Dear Folks, Hope this finds you all alright. I'm still kicking as usual…Your packages all arrived in fine shape. Was mighty glad to get them. All the presents were very much appreciated by myself and also my buddies.*
>
> *It was just three years ago yesterday that I enlisted in the Army. Sure never expected to say in this long. The way things are going, I'll be in at least two more years anyway.*
>
> *I haven't heard from Keith in a long time. I suppose he is in P.I. by now.*

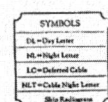

I've been expecting to hear that I'm an Uncle most anytime. I'm glad someone in the family can get the job done. It doesn't look like Keith or I will ever get around to it... Write when you have time.

Good Luck, Gerald

We received a telegram, dated February 4, saying Keith had been killed on December 20 on Leyte. The enemy surrounded his outfit, but Keith was not killed by enemy fire. He died instantly when he was hit by an airdrop of supplies. He was buried on Leyte, but was later moved to a military cemetery near Manila, where he still is.

After the war, we all decided we'd leave him buried there rather than bring him home. All magazine and newspaper reports at the time said the military cemeteries overseas were very well cared for. When Gerald came home he said he thought that was best. Besides, he said, in all that confusion of moving, how would you be sure you got the right body anyway? Gerald had been in a service squadron that helped load caskets on planes to come home, so we figured he knew best.

We later received the confirming letter, and during the summer we

CHAPTER 5 – *The War Years, 1941–1945*

France
March 6

Dear Folks

This is the first opportunity w had to write, in quite some time. I have been on the move again. I'm in France now, but can't say just where.

Hope this finds you folks all doing alright. I'm getting along fine myself.

Some of your mail caught up with me last night. I recieved the V-mail letter you wrote on the sixth of Feb., which told the sad news about Kieth. I can't say or do a thing that will make it any easier on you. You know how I feel so there is know use of me saying more. You did the right thing in sending a V-mail in stead of a cablegram. V-mail [arrives] much quicker.

Be [...]
APO [...]
partic[...]
write [...] often [...]
when you can. Good luck
Herald

PFC Herald Crofutt
SN 17029612
[...] Air Service Sqdr.
APO 374
[care] of P.M. N.Y. N.Y.

Mrs. John Bryant Sr.
Hat Creek
Wyoming

MAR 6
6 PM
1945
U.S. POSTAL SERVICE

PASSED
ARMY EXAMINER

received the few belongings he had, mostly pictures we had sent about things going on around home. His Purple Ribbon was sent to Lawrence, and his flag was sent to Gerald.

Keith had sent letters home as often as he could and we all wrote at least once a week. We treasured all his letters, and have them in the album with the ones we'd received from Gerald. They both treasured our letters, too, but couldn't carry them in combat. All letters from the front were censored. They just said "somewhere in the Pacific" or "somewhere in Africa."

After Keith's death and the death of a neighbor in the war, Gerald wrote to reassure us.

France, March 30, 1945, Dear Folks – You needn't worry about me. I'm not in the least bit of danger. Never have been and never will be as long as I stay with my present outfit...
Good Luck, Gerald

Gerald wrote us on April 29. On April 30, Hitler committed suicide. On May 7, Germany surrendered.

Germany, April 29, 1945 – Dear Folks, Just a few lines to let you know I am getting along all right. Hope this finds you all the same. We've been on the move again. I'm in Germany now and have been for quite some time. As far as I can see this country isn't any further advanced than any other old country over here, that I've been in.
Good Luck, Gerald

A few weeks later, the mail brought this letter.

Germany, May 12, 1945 – Dear Folks, How is the world treating all you people by this time? Ok I hope. I am still kicking, same as usual.
Now that all the celebrating is over, we're just sitting

around sweating out the next move. We don't know what they're going to do with us. It will probably be one of three things. We may go directly to China, back to the States for a while, or stay over here for the Army of occupation. Naturally, we all hope it's the States...I would like to see my two little nephews. Maybe teach them a few words. I'll bet they are plenty spoiled...

Good Luck, Gerald

In August, Gerald was still in Germany. In September, he was in France.

Lawrence volunteered into every branch of the service, even the Seabees, and never could pass the physical. He was disappointed not to get to go. Enis was called for his physical for the Army, but he never made it either. He felt left out, too.

We made it through the war years, keeping busy and writing letters to Gerald and Keith and any other soldiers we knew. We stayed out on the place, attending any "fund raisers" the different organizations put on in order to raise money for the Red Cross. I kept teaching in the local school.

We all did what volunteer work we could during the war. The government rationed gasoline, tires, sugar, coffee, shoes, canned goods, and so issued ration books for each. As each thing was to be rationed, I arranged for people in the neighborhood to register at the school. Eventually, even the 45-to 60-year-old men had to register for the draft and it saved them a trip to Lusk by registering at the school. School kids spent their savings on Savings Stamps, which they would stick in books. When the book was full they turned it in at the bank or post office for full value, plus interest.

In 1945, Lawrence and Tiny had a son, Charlie. Another son, Dave was born at Kremmling, Colorado in 1948.

Iris graduated from Lusk High School in 1945. That fall she taught three months at the Dixon-Swope School. It was so far out in the country and so isolated she decided to come back to the Ranger Hotel in Lusk to work. We were living in town then, too, and Glenn and Lola stayed with us in order to go to high school.

Glenn went to work at Culver's where he learned to weld. He bought a used bicycle and enjoyed riding it so much he bought one for Lola, too, and helped her learn to ride. They had baskets on the front. Glenn always took my little son George, who was two years old, riding in his basket.

In October 1945, Gerald was discharged from the Army Air Corps to come home. During his time in the military, he'd gone from Africa across Italy, where he'd contracted malaria. After spending some time on the island of Corsica for rest and recuperation, he went on into France and Germany.

Glenn gives my son George a ride, circa 1947.

Chapter 6
Finally...

The following year my family moved to Colorado. After his discharge, Gerald went to work at the Independent Refinery in Lusk, where he had been since he got out of the service. He and Iris rented a house in town, and kept Glenn and Lola so they could stay in high school. It was Gerald and Iris who helped Glenn and Lola finish high school. In 1948, Iris married Buck Baughn of Lance Creek and moved there.

Gerald bought a trailer house and kept Glenn until he graduated in 1950. Soon after that he went to work for Faye and Harry Baker out on their ranch at Lance Creek. In May 1951, Glenn married their daughter Shirlee.

Lola boarded with Mrs. Matthewson in town. She agreed to board girls for the $10 a month the district paid for country kids. In 1952, Lola graduated from high school. She sold tickets at the theater at night and worked as a nurses' aid at the hospital during the days. At that time she stayed in the nurses' quarters next to the hospital. In October 1952, she married Sam Leonard of Douglas and moved there.

In August of 1955, when Lola turned twenty-one, the estate was settled. No changes were made, there wasn't even a lot of money to inherit, the bills were all paid — we'd made it by all hanging together. We were fortunate there was nothing owing on the estate, just the small loan that Dad had gotten, and after sale of the calves every fall it was easy to make the payments on that loan. Enis was particularly helpful in that he stayed on the place and took care of the livestock. This provided money for the taxes and expenses on the place. My salary paid for food and clothing. We had lived there on the place for a number of years, but with marriages and jobs we eventually moved away.

That summer we had a family gathering and fenced the little graves. We didn't have new wiring for the fence, but put up what we had. Consequently, the livestock rubbed on it and it was in poor condition. So, in 1992, Iris and Buck, Enis and Barbara, Glenn and Shirlee took new material, a portable cement mixer, and welder over there. They set pipes in cement and welded new wire to them, made a gate and made cement markers to record dates of birth and death of each baby. They could not find the location of Ihla Faye's grave, so they added her stone to those of Lyle and Irma. They had a big sign made designating it "The Crofutt Family Cemetery." It is now listed in the Wyoming State Archives in Cheyenne, Wyoming.

The Bakers (Glenn's parents-in-law) eventually bought our homestead, so it

The Crofutt Family Cemetery on the homestead where the babies were buried. We fenced it in the early 1990s.

has stayed in the "family." After the Buena Vista School closed, the Bakers bought the building and added it onto the house the neighbors had built for us. So, the school where I taught, became part of the old homestead.

Looking Back

Looking back now on all those years, we had lots of tragedies, but we also had lots of blessings. We all graduated from high school. That doesn't seem like so much in the nineties, but in the thirties and forties that was quite an accomplishment, especially when we lived twenty-four miles from town. Over a span of twenty years, each year there was at least one, sometimes two or three Crofutts attending Lusk High School at the same time.

By the 1960s, we were mostly living near enough to each other that we took advantage of every holiday, birthday, or any other reason to all gather at one of the homes to visit. Everybody took food for dinner, and usually an early supper, too, before we all went home. There was always a game of canasta or pinochle going on.

One summer we had what we called "Work Day" Sundays. To start with John and I bought a place in Douglas. One requirement from the finance company was that we put a cement floor in the garage. It was suggested that we should get together and do that. The men brought a cement mixer and tools and did that, while the women prepared lunch.

We decided that we would all go to each place and to some job for them each week. At Iris and Buck's we plucked chickens for their freezer. At Glenn and Shirlee's we repaired their corral and loading chute. At Lola and Sam's we started painting their house, but it started to rain, so we had lunch and played pinochle. Enis was unmarried at that time, but he was on the ranch with Glenn, so it helped him to have the chute repaired.

We have all retired after busy lives. Some have moved to warmer climates, some are back in Lusk.

Lola and Sam live in a motorhome, so they have their "bed and breakfast" with them wherever they go. They built up a paving company, which they operated for years. After they sold it and bought the motorhome, they traveled all over the United States, Canada, and Mexico. They always make sure they are in San Diego, or some other warm place for the winter. They have three children—Ken, Tom and Sue.

Glenn and Shirlee retired to Springville, California. They have three children—Diane, Cheree (who graciously helped me edit this book), and Will. Another son, Michael, died in infancy and is buried at the foot of my parents' grave in the Lusk Cemetery.

Iris and Buck retired to Lusk since 1992. Previously, he had farmed in the Torrington area.

Enis married Barbara Towns in 1972. Enis had worked at the Story's for years, then he, Glenn and Shirlee bought and operated ranches in Niobrara County. Enis and Barbara now live in Douglas.

Lawrence and Tiny have two sons—Charlie and Dave. Dave has a son named after our brother Keith. Lawrence passed away on May 17, 1991. Graveside services were held on May 19 and he was buried in the Lusk Cemetery.

Gerald later moved Sacramento, California, where he worked for the California Highway Patrol. He married Marge Cezak, who had a daughter Dawn. After Marge's death he lived in Wyoming and Arizona for awhile. He became seriously ill with Alzheimer's and also had cancer. Dawn found a retirement home for him in Sacramento where he lived until his death in July 1986. He was buried there next to Marge.

John and I moved to the Ranger Apartments in Lusk in September 1995, after having lived in Riverton, WY for 25 years. We have one son, George. John passed away in May 1996 and is buried in the Lusk Cemetery.

One day, when my son George was in grade school, he asked if I knew they rationed things during the war. I said, "Oh yes. I have our ration books in the trunk. I'll get them out this afternoon." I thought that would be a good time to tell him about some of the hardships of war, until he asked, "Were you on the side of the North or the South?" He hadn't mentioned that they were studying the Civil War.

I have never at any time regretted helping the family, and they have more than made up for it by helping me in my later years, and I really appreciate that.

My siblings and me in 1997. Standing – Lola, Glenn, and Iris. Seated – Enis and me.